BROWNING AND MODERN THOUGHT

By the same Author

THE FUTURE OF POETRY
THE COUNTRY'S YEAR
FAREWELL TO TREES
AND OTHER POEMS

BROWNING AND MODERN THOUGHT

By

DALLAS KENMARE

HASKELL HOUSE PUBLISHERS LTD.
Publishers of Scarce Scholarly Books
NEW YORK. N. Y. 10012
1970

First Published 1939

HASKELL HOUSE PUBLISHERS LTD.
Publishers of Scarce Scholarly Books
280 LAFAYETTE STREET
NEW YORK, N. Y. 10012

Library of Congress Catalog Card Number: 76-117579

Standard Book Number 8383-1012-5

Printed in the United States of America

Dedication

"Dem seltenen Genie,
dem grossen Künstler,
dem guten Mensch"—
in thankfulness.

All we have willed or hoped or dreamed of good, shall exist;
Not its semblance, but itself; no beauty, nor good, nor power
Whose voice has gone forth, but each survives for the melodist
When eternity affirms the conception of an hour.
The high that proved too high, the heroic for earth too hard,
The passion that left the ground to lose itself in the sky,
Are music sent up to God by the lover and the bard;
Enough that he heard it once; we shall hear it by and by.

Abt Vogler.

CONTENTS

INTRODUCTION

THE tide of modernism sweeps on, bearing strange flotsam and jetsam. It is hard for the spectator to resist the flood, harder still for the critic, whose business it is to sift the mass carried along by the waters; almost impossible, it might seem, for the creative artist, who is faced with a problem similar in essence to the problem of the saint: to remain fully conscious of the tide of thought and action while remaining aloof from it. That degree of aloofness is as necessary for the artist as for the contemplative. The world and its Creator are in conflict: the world of men thrusts out God, while the love of God works continually to redeem the world. So the contemplative and the artist build a retreat where the voice of the world is silenced and the voice of reality heard. But—and here is the paradox—a ceaseless rhythm of mingling and withdrawal is essential. The saint cannot pray for the world until he knows the world, until he has allowed evil to draw near and so has seen exactly what it is he has to help to destroy; the artist cannot incarnate the beauty that is his reality until he has come to terms with ugliness. The effort to maintain the balance creates a tension that with many becomes intolerable, and chaos ensues. To live in the world, at one and the same time mistrusting and accepting it, is the gigantic task of the saint and the artist. There can be no permanent solution, but a measure of compromise must be achieved. There is no respite; there can be no final withdrawal; even when the inner refuge is entered, the world still clamours at the door, silenced only in certain rare moments. The measure in which the balance is successfully maintained is the measure of the man's greatness, for the artist and the saint who can live in the world, know the heart of humanity, learn the meaning of the behest "Resist not evil," and remain inviolate, has come to share in a certain infinitesimal degree something of the nature of God. And he can observe the flood of modernism dispassionately, noting the prevailing tendencies with the tolerant eye of a parent watching a child's experiments, and seeing in them an occasional germ of valuable development. Then he may sift the treasure from the rubbish, preserving through all his activities a centre that is unassailable.

In a mechanistic, largely materialistic age, which considers the soul a little out-of-date, and any mention of it more than a little embarrassing, it is natural that a supreme poet of the human soul should be misprised, and Browning at the present time certainly stands under the shadow of neglect. Yet it is strange that he should be assessed lower than Wordsworth, and disparagingly labelled Victorian, since clearly the work of Wordsworth is coloured by the influences of his period and often spoiled by Victorian sentimentality in a way that Browning's never is. In this book I shall attempt not only to re-establish Browning's position—once unquestioned—and prove his essential contact with modernity, but emphasize also the timeless quality of his work. Without this quality no poetry can be great. It is a test which, applied to contemporary poetry as a whole, rules out any claim it may make to immortality. Most modern poets make the mistake of living in the moment without realizing that this is no clue to happiness or wisdom unless the moment is related to the eternal, the sense of the eternal in the temporal continually preserved. Moreover, they find this particular moment in time unpleasant, and are so concerned with stressing its unpleasantness that they have no time to look for any possible significance in its evil. There is no forward direction; thus the prophetic element, another attribute of great poetry, is usually lacking.

The quality of the modern approach to art is unparalleled and its origin not easy to understand, although the Great War is usually held responsible for its inception. This explanation, like most easy explanations or generalisations, is not altogether to be trusted. It seems more likely that the war itself was a necessary and inevitable phase in the development of humanity, part of a lesson we are still far from having learned, and that the new movement in art is a part of this rhythm. Art, necessarily sensitive to every life-movement, reacts instantly to new pulsations. It is never safe to attribute any human reaction to *one* certain occurrence only. Mental processes are not so simple. In the history of the world, art is still only in its infancy, and the two thousand years of Christianity are but a moment. We are unavoidably apt to attach undue importance to the various movements that possess men's minds, finding it difficult, if not impossible, with our myopic vision, to relate them all to the greater whole which alone has final value. The extreme revulsion and nausea of the present phase may be an inevitable psychological perversion: not a turning from, but really a turning towards, beauty and reality. In some of the greatest poets we find this tendency at a certain stage of their development. The whole question is linked up with the artist's crucifixion in the world, and the descent into hell. At this moment we are awaiting the resurrection.

During the latter half of the last century also, a wave of materialism swept over England, and it is probably significant that Browning, outstanding as a Christian poet, flourished during an age of unbelief, as T. S. Eliot, another great Christian poet, flourishes to-day. During Browning's lifetime the thoughtful Englishman, perplexed by the pronouncements of Darwin, worried a great deal about the existence of God. In the third decade of the twentieth century, any such worry is often derided as childish: religious belief is reactionary now that the findings of psycho-analysis have at last revealed the true meaning of the desire for God, and the superman is he who is able to stand alone, without spiritual support from an imaginary father. The tendencies of modern thought place poetry, an interpretation of life, and therefore inextricably interwoven with religion, in a peculiar position. Life without God, poetry without religion, are contradictions in terms, so it is not surprising that comparatively few people to-day have any clear idea of what poetry is, and what it is trying to say. As a consequence, poetry itself suffers, stammering in confusion. The critic tries to help, the public grows impatient, and so long as the poet himself consents to a divorce from eternal values, this confusion must continue. He has lost the power to speak clearly.

In the midst of the inferno of conflicting beliefs there is a recall to religion, and the whole-hearted Christian (to be distinguished from the often half-hearted churchgoer) would suffer martyrdom for his belief that only Christianity can save civilization, and asks why it has never been given a fair trial. It is indeed possible that the prevalent confusion may be driving the civilized world to the only solution that has not yet been tried. Communism suggests one way, Fascism another. Both are headlong paths to destruction: both, by diametrically opposed ways, arrive at the same cul-de-sac: the abolition of personality. Only Christianity, which is concerned pre-eminently with the preservation and enlargement of personality, offers a solution. There is no other foundation on which it is safe to build, but it is natural that every other way should be tested first: truth is invariably arrived at not first, but last. The science of psycho-analysis, invaluable as a first step to self-knowledge, stops short exactly where Christianity begins.[1] The final analysis leads to self-abasement: man's noblest aspirations are "nothing but" varieties of infantile fixations, titanic efforts to compensate for deep-rooted deficiencies in the personality; in the last resort the enlightened subject has lost his inner life, and sees no way of saving it; he stands naked and ashamed before the final revelation, his loves, his ideals, his richest desires reduced to the whimperings of a pampered child incessantly scheming to attract attention. Conversely, Christianity, while fully recognizing man's weaknesses and follies, yet declares that he may attain to gigantic stature. It is the one great creed of self-development. But the present generation prefers psycho-analysis, and, reduced to so low an estimate of itself, logically must struggle and complain. There is a

[1] Since writing this, I have been interested to find similar views expressed by M. Nicolas Berdyaev in a book of inestimable value, *The Destiny of Man.* In the chapter on "Man" he gives a clear exposition of the relative virtues of Christianity and psychology.

fundamental blindness driving men to a preference for being cogs in a wheel rather than driving-forces themselves. Christianity values each individual man—"ye are of more value than many sparrows . . . the very hairs of your head are all numbered"—Communism and Fascism value him only as a cog in the social or national machine. The service of God is the only service that is freedom, yet men consent to slavery. Certainly the social system is bad, certainly it needs overturning; the Christian would be the first to agree that we are far from the Kingdom of Heaven, but no bloody revolution can save the world. That experiment has been tried too often, and never with success. The first Christians, having all things common, living in fellowship, in obedience to the command to love their neighbours as themselves, understood the only way to social salvation. Where the Christian ideal has been put into actual practice, success has followed. Here and there business concerns are run on Christian lines: the same ideal could be applied nationally, internationally, and England, Europe, and the world would move into an era of such prosperity and peace as it has never yet known. The prosperity would inevitably follow on the peace; progress is retarded solely by fear, mistrust, and lack of co-operation. There is no need for any other form of Socialism. Yet contemporary poets, as a whole, prefer the ideals of Communism, or some form of paganism, and even the leaders of religion seem uncertain of the best methods to convey their convictions. They incline to compromise; to attempt to make Christianity acceptable to the modern mind, when it would be better to suggest a study of Christianity of the kind that will readily be given to science or economics. It is a tragedy that Christianity shares with the works of Shakespeare a superficial familiarity, partly due to the inadequate teaching of childhood and school-days, which encourages the idea that further study is unnecessary. The glib quoting of a few texts, a few lines of Shakespeare—both usually misquoted—covers all the knowledge that appears to be desirable, and religion is usually the one subject the ignorant feel best qualified to discuss, because, since it has been taught them in childhood, it must be simple. In fact, it was remarked to me recently by an intelligent working-man that "you don't need brains for Bible study"—a dangerous half-truth.

There is urgent need to-day for a new approach to the whole subject, and a *practical* application of the principles of Christianity in a world long calling itself Christian. And the poets, the true builders, since they, like the prophets, build from the only enduring foundations, will be among the first to help.

CHAPTER 1

THE POET OF HUMANITY

THE demands of modernism in art appear to fall into three main categories:

(1) Realism.

(2) Ugliness.

(3) Obscurity.

The first category includes the preoccupation with the trivial, the transitory, and the topical, the implication being that other aspects of life, once considered vital, exist only in the imagination, and cannot therefore be classed as real. Many modernists appear to deny the validity of Keats's "truth of the imagination," confusing imagination, perhaps the most fruitful and valuable activity of the human mind, with the pastime of the mind known as fancy. But imagination reveals, while fancy conceals; imagination is concerned with truth, fancy often with falsity. And realism is actually in direct opposition to reality. A clearer definition of these familiar terms might be a healthy beginning to a better understanding of a subject on which scarcely anyone seems able to agree.

According to the modernist view, the minor events of daily life, even such intimate personal events as getting out of bed—or into it—bathing, dressing, eating, and so on, have a profound significance, also various domestic activities, such as bed-making, hanging washing out to dry, ironing, etc. This is "real"; this is life. It is important also to record conversations in suburban trains, boarding-house confidences, dance-hall chatter, in precise detail. In painting, this trend takes the form of those familiar works, exhibited, happily, in increasingly smaller numbers in the Royal Academy each year, of perspiring women stooping over ironing-boards, red-faced men in shirt-sleeves playing billiards, florid women hanging out washing in back gardens, and hot and irritable mothers and children waiting for excursion trains on dirty stations. These things are certainly aspects of life, but it would be hard to concede to them cosmic significance. This is not realism, but "actualism." The commonplace is not necessarily in itself pregnant with hidden values. It is conceivable that in future estimates of present-day art this period may be classified as the age of actualism, when the commonplace was exalted and the significant overlooked. It will be explained as the extreme of the reaction from Victorian sentimentality and flowery prettiness. A reaction was vitally necessary, but as yet the balance has not been attained, and modernism has swung as far from reality as the sentimentalists swung from realism. The great artist is concerned with the *whole* of life, not with certain aspects only. It is as false to stress only the trivialities as to ignore them altogether.

This applies equally to the prevalent pursuit of ugliness. Ugliness is "real"; beauty an illusion. Many modern poets deliberately avoid the least suggestion of beauty or romance in their writing, as if it were a menace to the ideal of truth. But *both* are aspects of life; dancing sunlight in spring trees no less real than a starving dog nosing about for food on a rubbish-dump. Modern poets as a whole would choose to write about the dog and the dump, with especial reference to the bony skeleton and shrivelled skin of the dog, rather than of the light and shadow quivering among the young leaves. Can no one explain why? No satisfactory explanation has yet been offered; it cannot be argued that starving dogs and rubbish-dumps exist, while spring sunlight and trees do not. If it is urged that the twentieth century is an age of ugliness, it can be claimed with equal truth that natural beauty remains unchanged, and that there can never be radical changes in the human heart, no matter how external conditions may alter. Different adjustments have to be made, but the flood-tide of human passions storms as dangerously, the inner response to romantic impulses is as swift and irresistible as in the Elizabethan age, nor has the soul ceased to hunger for completeness. It is the task of the poet to observe and record the significant; if he fail in this he should surrender any claim to greatness. He will therefore include the fact of beauty in a portrayal of life.

As for obscurity, is it conceivable that the truths the moderns have discovered are more difficult to convey than those revealed in the past by Shakespeare, Milton, Shelley—even Browning himself? These poets, in common with all writers, were no doubt aware of the inadequacy of words to embody their perceptions, but they finally overcame the hindrance comparatively successfully, even so far as to express some of the profoundest truths in the simplest language, so simple, in the case of Shakespeare, that many of his utterances have become "household words." There seems little hope that the involved lines of many modern writers will be quoted in three or four hundred years' time to clarify a difficulty, or give point to an argument.

However, on all these three counts: realism, ugliness and obscurity, it will not be difficult to prove Browning a master; in fact, literary criticism of the last century, and doubtless the opinion of the general reader also, condemned his work on those very charges, and not without some reason, although maturer consideration will withhold the condemnation. He was a supreme realist; his writing was often ugly, and it was unquestionably often obscure.

Browning was the great poet of human life. The study of humanity was with him a passion; sometimes, perhaps, a passion carried to excess, but without excess there is never genius. The great man learns eventually that he has no reason to fear his exuberance; the emotional reactions that are often derided as disproportionate, nor the moments of blinding light and abysmal despair. It may be years before the proper balance is attained, for, in the majority of cases, children showing signs of "peculiarity" are rigorously quelled, either by severity or ridicule, and taught to be ashamed of their dangerous reactions, not helped to channel and control them. However, the genius is not finally suppressible; sooner or later he will break through every kind of bondage, no matter what his early environment and its hampering effect on his developing personality. He himself, usually without human help, learns to value, to channel and to use those very reactions he was taught to mistrust and even to fear. It happens that Browning's childhood was happy and untrammelled; but he was in many ways an exception to the general rule; the early lives of most poets are notoriously unhappy and hedged about with environmental difficulties.

Due largely to a surface knowledge only of the principles of psychology, there is a considerable confusion of thought about human experience. It is often affirmed that everyone has similar experiences, and that therefore "disproportionate" reactions to these experiences should be suppressed and overcome. This is to misunderstand completely the infinite variety of reactions, varying in quality, depth and intensity, possible to different types of personalities.

Mr. Middleton Murry refers to this in his introductory essay to the new edition of *Things to Come:* human reaction to experience is as various as human faces, no two can be alike. To put the case simply: it is as if every individual were given a certain musical theme, a simple tune consisting of a few notes only, to work out in his own way. Some have only the ability to compose a nursery-rhyme tune, some a sonata, but the genius cannot choose but labour, with proportionate pain and joy, to create a symphony. The main theme: birth, love, death, is common to every man living; it remains for each individual to make what he must of the theme. Therefore, if Browning saw in all the faces in the street "masks of divinity," as G. K. Chesterton says, we cannot condemn this as extravagant, since those who have in any degree the quality of greatness are apt to assume that all other men are great, the intensity of their own imagination creating far more than actually exists. But this is not an error to be condemned; it has an element of divinity. It may often lead to danger, almost certainly to disillusionment, and is a frequent source of embarrassment and final exasperation to those incapable of understanding, but there is no blame; the trouble is that the reactions of the genius cannot be pressed into the meagre mould of everyday life. Possibly his value in human affairs is similar to the achievement of Pippa in *Pippa Passes;* unrecognized, a divine messenger passes by, and those whom he has touched in passing will never be quite the same again. There is tragic truth in William Sharp's cynical remark that the poet is too ready to write a sonnet to Helen when Helen is in fact only Nellie, and would be more pleased with the gift of a pair of gloves.

The fact that Browning was the great poet of human life, second in this only to Shakespeare, accounts for the realism, ugliness and obscurity in his work, because clearly human life includes all this: there are shallows as well as depths, often it is hideous, cruel and crude, certainly darkly obscure, confusing and enigmatic. Browning was a relentless realist. He had no use for sentimentalizing, or for a delicate, and so untrue, veiling of facts. Take for example *Soliloquy of the Spanish Cloister*, or *The Laboratory*, poems of pure hate, or *Fra Lippo Lippi*, a poem psychologically faultless, which might be quoted by a psycho-therapist to prove the perils of sexual repression, or *Porphyria's Lover*, another psychological poem of a curious type of abnormality. Because Browning was healthy-minded, pure in heart, he had no need to cloak or veil what are called "the facts of life" (as if there were no important facts other than sexual). Entirely free of Victorian "delicacy," and because he was a profoundly religious man, he feared no aspect of truth, and recorded his perceptions of evil and sin as honestly as his intuitions of beauty. Only the impure fear truth; the saint faces vice undismayed, seeing only with the eye of compassion. On this count alone it would be difficult to label Browning Victorian. He was as honest as Shakespeare. And possibly only those whose lives have been near shipwreck through the vice of discreet evasion will fully value such honesty, since only they can rightly assess its essential purity, and, conversely, the impurity of so-called discretion.

But the poet of human life will not stress the physical and material aspects alone; this is where many of the modernists are mistaken. Life includes soul as well as body. In *Fifine at the Fair*, for example, there is much beauty, of a typically Browningesque kind:

Fettered, I hold my flower, her own cup's weight would
    win
From off the tall slight stalk a-top of which she turns
And trembles, makes appeal to one who roughly earns
Her thanks instead of blame, (did lily but know),
By thus constraining length of lily, letting snow
Of cup-crown, that's her face, look from its guardian stake.

And, in addition to brilliant pen-pictures of fair-life, as vivid in their way as the paintings of Laura Knight, coupled with profound metaphysical reflections, there are many passages similar to this:

You draw back skirts from filth like her
Who, possibly, braves scorn, if, scorned, she minister
To age, want, and disease of parents one or both;

Nay, peradventure, stoops to degradation, loth
That some just-budding sister, the dew just on the rose,
Should have to share in turn the ignoble trade—who
knows?

Ay, who indeed! Myself know nothing, but dare guess
That off she trips in haste to hand the booty . . . yes,
'Twixt fold and fold of tent, there looms he, dim-discerned,
The ogre, lord of all those lavish limbs have earned
-Brute-beast-face- ravage, scar, scowl and malignancy.

Typically, this poem is inclusive, ranging from darkness to light, ugliness to beauty, triviality to profundity, with equal ease.

At some period in the development of human thought it was suggested that the poet deals in dreams only, and, since the idea is false, it has naturally grown to gigantic proportions. The world is an admirable forcing-house for false theories. In *Fifine at the Fair* Browning refutes this idea:

A poet never dreams;
We prose-folk always do: we miss the proper duct
For thoughts on things unseen, which stagnate and
obstruct
The system. . . .
. . . What ghosts do poets see,
What demons fear? what man or thing misapprehend?

The poets are the true realists; by virtue of their calling they cannot choose but see reality, not only realism, and are fitted for the task through the high degree of development of the intuitive faculty which sees "things unseen." This faculty is akin to the perfect sight of the Divine Man, who "saw what was in man," "perceived their thoughts," and was the world's greatest realist. Yet it is usually assumed that only the type known in psychology as the extravert faces facts and understands the real needs of men. This because the "tough-minded man," to use William James's definition, is able, through lack of imagination, to rush in where the angel would not presume to tread, and by sheer force of personality and the strength derived from the inability to see beyond the obvious, contrives to carry through a difficult situation successfully, where the sensitive man, confused by his capacity for seeing all sides to the problem, existent and potential, would be paralysed almost at the outset. It is because the extravert does *not* understand life that action is to him easy. He not only does not understand it; he cannot realize there is anything to understand. This, of course, is not his fault; psychological differences are as fundamental and ineradicable as the physiological. The influence of the "tough-minded" is easily seen, while the influence of the artist can scarcely ever be immediately apparent; it is slow in action, but profound and far-reaching. This is why I argue elsewhere [1] that Shelley, as passionate poet-reformer, cannot be said to be *directly* responsible for

[1] *The Future of Poetry.*

the adoption of the reforms he urged. The influence is indirect: the reforming, transforming thought of the poet soaks into men's minds slowly, imperceptibly, and eventually, perhaps only after a long period of time, incites to action. It is the grain of mustard seed, the leaven pregnant with hidden power. The conclusions the artist arrives at have been reached by the hardest of paths. Every experience has been essentially experimental, no matter how deeply his emotions are involved. Thus

> the failure of his experiment . . . does not involve the failure of his life. For the aspect of life which implicated his soul would be his understanding of life, and, to the understanding, defeat is no less interesting than victory.[1]

Defeat, in fact, may be even more interesting; it certainly demands closer thought. Success is apt to be accepted thoughtlessly, but it is impossible not to reflect on the meaning of failure. The problem of failure, in its many varying forms, never gives the man of imagination a moment's rest, and it is the contemplation of its significance that finally gives him power. Browning is pre-eminently the poet of triumphant failure; that he is the great poet of courage naturally follows. He saw life always as a battle-ground, where the soul is tested, and often tortured, in the cause of development:

[1] Walter Lippmann, *A Preface to Morals*.

When the fight begins within himself
A man's worth something. . . .

. . . .

. . . the soul wakes
And grows. Prolong that battle through his life!
Never leave growing till the life to come![1]

While he is striving always "not to remake himself, but to make the absolute best of what God made," there can never be ultimate failure. God considers not results, but motives.

The experiences of a long life—and we know that to a poet of Browning's calibre even the smallest experience can be pregnant with significance—rather than having the power to diminish his ardent courage and belief, increased it, until at the last, in the last words he ever wrote, he proclaimed the joy and triumph of marching "breast forward never doubting clouds would break," and ever asserted that we "fall to rise, are baffled to fight better." In this poem, *Asolando*, written when Browning was seventy-seven, and published on the day he died, there is a certain affinity with the last and greatest work of another poet: Robert Bridges's *Testament of Beauty*. Though wholly different in matter and manner, both are effective replies to the view that all is vanity, and old age bitter, rather suggesting that as the physical

[1] *Bishop Blougram's Apology.*

powers wane the spiritual powers increase, and that the years, rather than diminishing the poet's powers, deepen and enrich them. Such poets as Browning and Bridges refute the common idea of time as an enemy; it can take from them nothing that cannot be given back in another form, enriched a hundredfold.

> " The Poet's age is sad: for why?
> In youth the natural world could show
> No common object but his eye
> At once involved with alien glow—
> His own soul's iris-bow.
>
> " And now a flower is just a flower;
> Man, bird, beast are but beast, bird, man—
> Simply themselves, uncinct by dower
> Of dyes which, when life's day began,
> Round each in glory ran." [1]

The answer is that the clearer apprehensions of age reveal the very naked beauty of God's creation, undimmed by the veil, although a lovely shimmering veil, the ardours of youth inevitably draw about every scene. No doubt the cooler temper of age discloses much which the wild emotions of youth and the confusions of the middle years conceal.

Browning neither exalted nor disparaged the body; his was the attitude of the eminently sane, and, again, the truly religious, man. Although he asked:

[1] *Prologue to Asolando.*

Thy body at its best,
How far can that project thy soul on its lone way? [1]

in the same poem he urged:

Let us not always say
"Spite of this flesh to-day
I strove, made head, gained ground upon the whole!"
As the bird wings and sings,
Let us cry "All good things
Are ours, nor soul helps flesh more, now than flesh helps
soul."

The body can be an enemy to be wrestled with and overcome; in itself it cannot perhaps greatly help the progress of the soul, yet it can provide some of life's keenest joys:

Oh, our manhood's prime vigour!
No spirit feels waste,
Not a muscle is stopped in its playing nor sinew unbraced.
Oh, the wild joys of living! the leaping from rock up to
rock,
The strong rending of boughs from the fir-tree, the cool
silver shock
Of the plunge in a pool's living water, the hunt of the bear
And the sultriness showing the lion is couched in his
lair. . . .

. . . .

How good is man's life, the mere living! how fit to employ
All the heart and the soul and the senses forever in joy! [2]

[1] *Rabbi Ben Ezra.*
[2] *Saul.*

This is supreme physical satisfaction, yet in the same poem David says:

Leave the flesh to the fate it was fit for! the spirit be thine!
By the spirit, when age shall o'ercome thee, thou still shalt
enjoy
More indeed, than at first when inconscious, the life of
a boy.

Browning's attitude to the physical was the reverse of Victorian. His own intense vitality and virility sprang largely from his joy in physical life, "the mere living." And despite the spiritual content of his poetry, it has none of the attenuated spirituality, divorced from earth, that can mar great poetry of a certain type. Human life was more to Browning than a supersensuous existence of the spirit alone; indeed, he would fiercely have denied the possibility or desirability of such a life on earth.

Not a muscle is stopped in its playing, nor sinew unbraced.
Oh, the *wild* [1] joys of living. . . .

It was this "wildness," this sense of continual excitement and delight, that made him the true mystic, who saw God not only in His heaven, but in every bush and flower and human face. His joy was worship, and it was his vision of God that made of living so vivid and purposeful an adventure. Possibly he never had to learn the balance, often so difficult, of body, soul

[1] The italics are mine.

and mind; certain individuals are able to live in the three worlds simultaneously, without discomfort, appreciating the value of all the elements that make up man's nature. This does not mean that there are no difficulties; the genius has conflicts and difficulties of adjustment which, by virtue of his type, assume gigantic proportions, but he possesses pre-eminently the gift of unification.

Shelley saw the world as a purgatory to be endured, and although his own personal experience tragically justified him in the belief, he never lost faith in the ultimate possible perfectibility of man, and never ceased to work for that ideal. Yet there is a grain of truth in Matthew Arnold's sweeping criticism of him as an "ineffectual angel beating in the void his luminous wings in vain," for he never could adjust himself completely to a world unready for angels, and in that sense beat his wings wildly and vainly in the void of an unregenerate world. Browning, however, saw life with relentless clarity. He recognized the impossibility of immediate reform, and therefore continued to fulfil the purposes of his own being without undue concern for the ultimate result. There is no doubt that he realized at a very early stage in his development a truth which usually dawns considerably later: the artist has a part to play which he cannot choose but accept, but he will not further his cause by setting out with deliberate intent to reform humanity; such an intention invariably defeats its own ends, and the baffled artist-reformer retreats wounded and bleeding from the fray. Humanity refuses to be thus directly helped; is inclined rather to resent interference, so the end must be attained by more indirect means. It cannot be said that any of Browning's poetry is written with intent to reform. He wrote because he had to write, and was fortunate in escaping the conflict with family influences and environment that so often delays an artist's development by many years. No false steps in youth hampered him; so far as we know, no opposition. His genius was allowed to develop unchecked; he was not hindered by parents who decide that the son must naturally follow the father's calling, as if a child were no more than a replica of the parent. In fact, his early life refutes the common theory that conflict with environment and circumstances is the best goad to achievement. It seems that such theories have their roots in the more destructive types of Christian beliefs, which have exalted the life of difficulty and pain as an end in itself, not a means to an end. The influence of these beliefs is far-reaching. Beauty is associated with sensuality; the pleasant can never be the good; the happy life must be the wrong life, and unless duty has an element of distaste it cannot be the true duty. Manifestations of joy are regarded with suspicion. It cannot have occurred to the followers of this type of belief that God is asked to "make His chosen people *joyful*," that we are enjoined to "rejoice in the Lord alway," that the Gospel of Jesus is pre-eminently a gospel of joy, because it is the gospel of true life. Jesus was the soundest of psychologists: he worked from within outwards; he knew where sin and disease had their origin, knew also the close affinity between the two, and that the perfect life is inevitably the life of joy:

> These things have I spoken unto you that My joy might remain in you, and that your joy might be full. . . .
>
> Your joy no man taketh from you.[1]

This joy may be interpreted as blessedness, a state far removed from the "happiness" which is usually demanded as if it were a right. It is the plain truth that the wholehearted Christian has found a joy no man can take from him, independent of external events. But he has ceased to think of "happiness." It was this Christian joy that caused Paul and Silas when cast into prison to sing praises to God, which furthermore impelled Paul to say:

> And now, behold, I go bound in the spirit unto Jerusalem, not knowing the things that shall befall me there: save that the Holy Ghost witnesseth in every city, saying that bonds and afflictions abide me. But none of

[1] *Gospel according to St. John* xv. 11 and xvi. 24.

these things move me, neither count I my life dear unto myself, so that I might finish my course with *joy*, and the ministry, which I have received of the Lord Jesus, to testify the Gospel of the grace of God.[1]

There is a certain affinity between Browning and St. Paul; both were essentially robust and healthy-minded visionaries, ever ready to affirm the joy of the Christian life. Neither was concerned overmuch with renunciation, mortification, or the more negative aspects of goodness, preferring to stress the creative quality of suffering, the joy to be found in sorrow gladly endured as a means to an end. Both invariably saw suffering as a working-through to joy, not as an end in itself. This is as it were the gospel of the Resurrection rather than the gospel of the Crucifixion. No doubt, had Browning been a material instead of a spiritual builder, he would have built the Church of the Risen Christ, or had he been a painter, he would have delighted in portraying the appearances on and after Easter Day rather than the scene on Calvary.

It was Browning's belief in the supremacy of spiritual values that made him the poet of glorious failure. Nowhere in his work is there any suggestion that the short-sighted view of life ever for a moment blinded him. Present evil must always be for some future good; the truth is clouded, but only tem-

[1] *Acts of the Apostles* xx. 24.

porarily, time will reveal the meaning, and the joy to which the suffering was leading.

All we have willed or hoped or dreamed of good, shall exist,
Not its semblance, but itself; no beauty, nor good, nor
power
Whose voice has gone forth, but each survives for the
melodist
When eternity affirms the conception of an hour.
The high that proved too high, the heroic for earth too
hard,
The passion that left the ground to lose itself in the sky
Are music sent up to God by the lover and the bard;
Enough that he heard it once: we shall hear it by and by.

Here, in this stanza of *Abt Vogler*, is the answer to those who imagine that because Browning had an outwardly easy life he can have known nothing of frustration and failure. No wonder, then, they argue, that he was able to write optimistic poetry, write so glibly of the bitterness of failure and its true meaning, when he himself had never experienced it. The answer is in the line:

The high that proved too high, the heroic for earth too
hard.

Because Browning was a spiritual Titan it naturally follows that the successes and failures he counted as real existed in the realm of spiritual values alone, and were of gigantic proportions. All was for him "heroic, for earth too hard." Every word he wrote carries its own evidence. An apparently comfortable, untroubled man of the world, perfectly at ease in social life, in later years an outstanding social success, he yet had no true existence in this surface life at all; he lived it easily because for him it had no final value; to him it was as simple as an elementary addition sum to a great mathematician. This commonplace life of every day demands less than nothing from a man of Browning's stature; he is an adult among children, Gulliver among the Lilliputians, no effort is needed to live among so-called adults whose mental development is too often arrested in adolescence. The proportion of human beings who attain to full mental and spiritual maturity is startingly small, hence all the tragedy in our fallen world.

Possibly it was because Browning asked nothing from the material world that it gave him so much, because he was cast for an altogether different drama that materially he suffered not at all; his energies were all required elsewhere. When in *Christmas Eve* he exclaims:

How very hard it is to be
A Christian! Hard for you and me,
—Not the mere task of making real
That duty up to its ideal,
Effecting thus, complete and whole,
A purpose of the human soul—
For that is always hard to do;
But hard, I mean, for me and you

To realize it, more or less,
With even the moderate success
Which commonly repays our strife
To carry out the aims of life,

we realize the reality of his own personal struggle. It is, of course, evident throughout his poetry. Nor is it possible to think that a man to whom the religious life had always been easy would have been able to write *Bishop Blougram's Apology*. His courage is reflected in the lines:

What matter though I doubt at every pore,
Head-doubts, heart-doubts, doubts at my fingers' ends,
Doubts in the trivial life of every day,
Doubts at the very bases of my soul
In the grand moments when she probes herself—
If finally I have a life to show.

"In the *grand* moments when she probes herself"—those are the moments the lesser man fears, and will go to almost any lengths to avoid. And this fear, this timorous avoidance, is at the root of psychological breakdown and disaster.

It is easy, again, to argue that the opinions and emotions expressed in the *Dramatic Monologues*, and in much of his writing, are not Browning's own. The answer is that the creative artist cannot create from ignorance, and that at some time in his experience, perhaps for a fleeting moment only, he must have felt the emotion he portrays, must have fully grasped the point of a certain argument. Every human attribute exists in its potentiality in every human being; in some, certain qualities develop, in others, entirely different ones, and in the creative artist, consciousness is so heightened, and the degree of every quality so greatly magnified, that no more than a momentary flash of the meaning of evil may reveal the whole extent and depth of evil in human life; in that moment he has explored darknesses and depths unguessed by others in a whole lifetime of experience. It is a matter of the degree of consciousness. Possibly only the profoundly religious man is capable of apprehending evil, just as only the truly blessed man understands sorrow, and has no choice but to work to alleviate it.

So Browning, from the outset a successful poet and an unusually well-adjusted human being, is the great poet of failure because his true life was not in the world of material values at all, but in the realm of spiritual values. And that is where the grimmest battles are fought, not on the Stock Exchange. That is where, paradoxically, there is eternal success and hourly failure. Browning was born a Christian; quite early in his life he must have recognized his purpose. Stopford Brooke says:

> He dedicated himself to the picturing of humanity; and he came to think that a Power beyond ours had accepted this dedication, and directed his work. He . . . felt a Hand "always above my shoulder." . . . And he believed

that he had certain God-given qualities which fitted him for this work.[1]

It naturally follows that he understood Christian values instinctively:

> A man's life consisteth not in the abundance of things he possesseth. . . .
>
> . . . .
>
> It is harder for a camel to go through the eye of a needle than for a rich man to enter the Kingdom of God.
>
> . . . .
>
> Take no thought for the morrow, what ye shall eat and what ye shall drink. . . .

Hard sayings these for the materialist; never hard or dark for the spiritual man. Browning no doubt cared as little for possessions as St. Francis of Assisi, but accepted them as a matter of course rather than risk valuable time in overturning the material conditions of his life in order to live—somewhat quixotically—in harmony with his true beliefs. His purpose was so urgent that he needed every moment to fulfil it, and any outward disturbance of his life would have been a hindrance he could not allow.

Again and again he stresses the value of a purpose, and of the significance of effort in itself:

[1] *The Poetry of Robert Browning.*

But try . . . the trying shall suffice;
The aim, if reached or not, makes great the life:
Try to be Shakespeare, leave the rest to fate! [1]

Strive, and hold cheap the strain;
Learn, nor account the pang; dare, never grudge the throe! [2]

What I aspired to be
And was not, comforts me.[3]

In *Rabbi Ben Ezra* he writes of love and power in a way which foreshadows his reflections on the same theme in his last work, *Asolando*, published twenty-five years later:

I see the whole design,
I, who saw power, see now love perfect too;
Perfect I call Thy plan:
Thanks that I was a man;[4]

Power is love—transports, transforms
Who aspired from worst to best. . . .

I have faith such end shall be:
From the first, Power was—I knew.
Life has made clear to me
That, strive but for closer view,
Love were as plain to see.[5]

1 *Bishop Blougram's Apology.*
2 *Rabbi Ben Ezra.*
3 *Ibid.*
4 *Ibid.*
5 *Asolando.*

In passing, it is noteworthy that this section of *Asolando*, "Reverie," is a significant poem for a man so near the end of life to have written:

> I know there shall dawn a day
> —Is it here on homely earth?
> Is it yonder, worlds away,
> Where the strange and new have birth,
> That Power comes full in play
>
> . . . .
>
> Somewhere, below, above,
> Shall a day dawn—this I know—
> When Power, which vainly strove,
> My weakness to o'erthrow,
> Shall triumph. I breathe, I move,
>
> I truly am, at last!
> For a veil is rent between
> Me and the truth which passed
> Fitful, half-guessed, half-seen,
> Grasped at—not gained, held fast.

Rabbi Ben Ezra is the triumphant poem of old age, written when Browning was old enough to have reflected much on its meaning. The later years, the Rabbi says, are happier than the uncertain years of youth, when man looks for and demands so much and consequently finds so little (treasures are found only when they are no longer sought). As time passes, peace comes: the years of fever give place to the years of quiet contemplation, and slowly but surely life's plan begins to show: true values are established, again the unworthiness of the world's judgment is stressed, and the necessity for all experience, no matter how painful, how almost impossible to understand or to bear, is appreciated as vital to the soul's development. And it is in age that the true relation between soul and body is understood at last. Since in this life the soul can only be manifested through the body, to despise the flesh must be wrong. This, again, is the profoundly Christian view: the temple of the Holy Spirit is worthy of honour, and must not be abused or scorned. The poem ends on the note of complete acceptance:

My times be in Thy hand!
Perfect the cup as planned!
Let age approve of youth, and death complete the same!

And in *Asolando*, as in *La Saisiaz* written eleven years earlier, when Browning was actually old in years, he reiterated this philosophy.

Saul is perhaps pre-eminently the poem of failure and triumph. Again Browning powerfully affirms his belief in the value of the struggle as opposed to the apparent result. Because David has done all in his power to help the King he cannot know despair, even though he fail in his mission. His own service is perfect, his soul at peace, because of the perfection of his endeavour:

. . . What stops my despair?
This:—'tis not what man does that exalts him, but what man would do!
See the King—I would help him, but cannot, the wishes fall through.

Could I wrestle to save him from sorrow, grow poor to enrich,
To fill up his life, starve my own out, I would—knowing which,
I know that my service is perfect. . . .

Saul is an outstanding poem. There is a beauty and virility, a quality of inspiration, rare even in Browning, as if the poem had written itself. From beginning to end it sweeps along in a smooth-flowing, inevitable metre to which the regular rhyme and rhythm is integral: a good example of the success of the perfect rhymed poem, where the rhyme is inwoven with the thought as the body with the soul. Another good example is Meredith's *Love in the Valley*, where a rhyme-scheme which in a lesser poet's hands would prove exasperating is used with consummate success. The modernists who deliberately exclude rhyme overlook a vital and mysterious fact: that a poem chooses its own form, and will not accept a form *chosen for it* by the writer. It has a mysterious life and will of its own.

Saul also celebrates the glory of the love of friendship, a subject on which too little has been written.

The emotion expressed in the words: "Very pleasant hast thou been unto me: thy love to me was wonderful, passing the love of women" is habitually misunderstood and misprised, and often neglected even by the poets. Its value was best appreciated perhaps by D. H. Lawrence, who constantly affirmed his belief in the necessity for a perfect relationship between people of the same sex. At its best it can be as inspiring and strength-giving as any love-relationship: the use of the word " love" here betrays its unfortunate limiting in modern usage, which suggests that love is confined to sexual emotion only. Particularly in recent years, a superficial knowledge of various perversions has proved extremely harmful. Many of these perversions are admittedly not fully understood even by medical psychologists, and it would probably be safer for the public to have no knowledge at all than the surface knowledge that prevails at present. Such a book, for example, as *The Romantic Agony* by Mario Praz is safe only in the hands of readers with a wide and profound understanding of abnormal psychology. The harm that can be done to the uninitiated is incalculable, which is of course true of the science of psychology as a whole: a thoughtless acceptance of Freudian theories is apt to be too quickly seized upon. To believe that every kind of human love is "nothing but" a variation of the sex-instinct is too easy a dismissal of a profound problem. The " nothing but" theory is of all generalizations perhaps the most pernicious. The ignorant man is always the man who glibly labels a condition or a situation; the man of wide knowledge and experience suspends judgment until he has weighed and considered all the known aspects and possibilities, and even then hesitates to speak with final authority.

The theme and the treatment of *Saul* should prove an effective refutation of the idea that sexual love alone inspires man to his highest achievements. David's striving is for an end no less than the saving of a soul from despair, and the revelation necessary is given to him in proportion to his need. The Old Testament story says simply, in its sublimely unadorned language:

> And David came to Saul, and stood before him, and he loved him greatly. . . . And it came to pass, when the evil spirit from God was upon Saul, that David took the harp and played with his hand: so Saul was refreshed, and was well, and the evil spirit departed from him.[1]

"He loved him greatly." The power of this love, and the healing power of music, wrought the miracle at last.

In *Easter Day* Browning says: "Too much love there can never be," and in *A Soul's Tragedy:*

> My soul's capacity for love widens—needs more than one object to content it, and, being better instructed, will

[1] I *Samuel* xvi. 23.

not persist in seeing all the component parts of love in what is only a single part—nor in finding that so many and so various loves are all united in the love of a woman—manifold uses in one instrument. . . . Love is a very compound thing. . . .

The wide capacity for love is an essential quality of the artist, who finds himself continually baffled by the narrow views of the world. The universal love which sees all men as God's creations is a concept so integral to the Christian faith that hate becomes impossible. There is no "virtue" in loving; the emotion is inevitable. This does not mean, however, that the dark demons cease to make assaults on the soul. In the genius the reason for his expansive love is explained largely by the infinite variety of his own nature, which impels him to search constantly for satisfaction for all the different, sometimes conflicting, aspects. The various relationships, and various people, are really aspects of himself, as in dreams the chief characters are aspects of the dreamer. When the genius happens to be an avowed Christian also, the extent and scope of the love-passion is further increased, and its depth and intensity explained by his inevitable exuberance and so-called extravagance. Half-measures, compromise, a lukewarm attitude to life, all are impossible to him, since they are a denial of truth. And it is well to remember that no great work is achieved without passion, an intensity burning not necessarily with an outward flame, but at white heat within. One of the major problems of the artist's life consists in learning to channel his overflowing love and vivid life-consciousness. It must be poured into suitable vessels, and most are far too small to receive and contain it. After a series of painfully unsuccessful experiments he realizes that, having failed in the attempt to "live poetry" the only alternative is to control the flood rigidly in actual living, and allow it to flow at full tide only in his art. This, to the Christian, seems a direct violation of his principles: he cannot reconcile the realization of failure with his knowledge of love as the supreme healing power. The problem is vast and profound; there is no easy solution, since every form of divine love is un-at-home in our fallen world. We know that even with Jesus the swift-flowing river of his love was turned back upon him, and for love he was crucified. "The whole world lieth in the hand of the Evil One." But Browning constantly affirms that there can be no ultimate failure so long as the motive has been pure.

Browning's first published poem, *Pauline*, which appeared when he was twenty-one, reveals his insatiable thirst for life, and his essentially mystical understanding of love.

I am made up of an intensest life,
Of a most clear idea of consciousness
Of self. . . .

. . . a principle of restlessness
Which would be all, have, see, know, taste, feel, all. . .

. . . .

I cannot chain my soul, it will not rest
In its clay prison, this most narrow sphere;
It has strange powers and feelings and desires,
Which I cannot account for nor explain,
But which I stifle not, being bound to trust
All feelings equally, to hear all sides,
Yet I cannot indulge them, and they live,
Referring to some state or life unknown.

. . . .

What I feel may pass all human love,
Yet fall far short of what my love should be.

. . . .

I have made life my own
I would not be content with all the change
One frame could feel, but I have gone in thought
Through all conjecture. . . .

. . . .

I can live all the life of plants, and gaze
Drowsily on the bees that flit and play,
Or bare my breast for sunbeams which will kill,
Or open in the night of sounds, to look
For the dim stars; I can mount with the bird. . . .

. . . .

Or like a fish breathe-in the morning air
In the misty sun-warm water. . . .

. . . .

But my soul saddens when it looks beyond;
I cannot be immortal nor taste all.

It remains one of the baffling problems in literary criticism why this first poem of Browning's should always be referred to somewhat apologetically. Never has a poem been so damned with faint praise. Possibly Browning's own feeling for it in later years largely accounts for the critics' universal apathy. But quite apart from the fact that the writer was a boy of only twenty, the matter, form, diction, beauty and power of the work are outstanding, nor is the influence of Shelley, so invariably stressed, by any means self-evident. Actually, Browning was too much an individualist to remain long under the influence of another writer. This quality in the artist is not due to arrogance, but to his own overmastering separateness of being. A Browning is inevitably a Browning, and never an echo of another poet. It sometimes happens that two artists find themselves on almost identical ground, having independently and unknown to each other arrived at similar conclusions. Then critics and public immediately deduce that they are mutually "influenced," or that one is the disciple of the other. The truth is that although the knowledge of thought-sympathy and unity of aim proves a powerful revitalizing influence and source of strength, the two remain inevitably individuals, and cannot, if they be great artists, choose but express their own personal reactions in their own way, nor would they wish to if they could. Actual personal experience is too valuable to be set aside, and no creative artist would wish to be nothing more than the echo of another, no matter how deeply that other might be loved and valued. Too much stress is laid on influences. It is unlikely that any intelligent reader of Browning and Shelley would observe a Shelleyan influence unless taught to look for it by the critics. Moreover, as I have pointed out earlier, there are certain radical temperamental differences in the two poets.

Almost the entire range and scope of Browning's later art is foreshadowed in *Pauline*. As a poem prophetic of the writer's future it is unique in literature. Here is the desire for experience of every kind, later manifested in his unique preoccupation with humanity, reflected in *Men and Women*, *Dramatis Personæ*, *Dramatic Monologues*, everywhere throughout his work; the passion for philosophy, the intensity of religious feeling, and innate mysticism:

> And what is it that I hunger for but God?
> My God, my God, let me for once look on thee
> As though nought else existed, we alone!

the powerful capacity for, and understanding of, human love, the desire for spiritual power, the belief in the ultimate victory despite the appearance of failure:

> . . . this song shall remain to tell for ever
> That when I lost all hope of such a change,
> Suddenly beauty rose on me again,

also his embracing love of nature, and gift for nature-writing. All these qualities, developed and expanded illimitably throughout his life, are suggested in his first published poem. It towers above the earliest work of any other poet, and Browning's own later contempt for it is not easy to understand. It cannot have been his cool critical faculty alone that caused him to lash his first-born. However, only the poet himself can know why certain work comes to seem intolerable; his reactions are connected with all kinds of personal reasons which inevitably remain hidden from outsiders.

The passion for humanity, the unfailing fascination for him of human character and dramatic situations, found expression in innumerable poems, dramas, studies, until thirty-five years after the publication of *Pauline*, his greatest work, *The Ring and the Book*, appeared, and although he continued to write for the remaining twenty years of his life, there is no doubt that this work marks the peak of his achievement, and seems to divide his artistic development into two definite periods. It is as if here his passion for truth reached its focal point. G. K. Chesterton has said of him that "in all his life . . . he tried always the most difficult things" [1] and certainly the search for truth is the most difficult, and the most dangerous, task that can be attempted. It leads not only into every conceivable kind of actual situation, but also into laby-

[1] G. K. Chesterton, *Robert Browning*.

rinths of thought that can verge on insanity. It means a consideration not of the thing seen but of the thing unseen, of which the seen is only the covering, as the body of the soul; contemplation not of the thing said, but of the thing unsaid, not the words heard, but the unheard thoughts underlying the words. In short, it aims at the impossible, for we move in so dark a forest of illusion, the final truth and meaning of personality and action hidden even from ourselves, that the writer who is preoccupied with this particular aspect of human life is doomed to recurrent desperation and even despair. Certainly Browning comes nearer to a solution than any other poet, and in *The Ring and the Book*, where the same situation is seen through the eyes of the different characters in the drama, and also by various others, we realize to what heights and depths, lengths and confusions this pursuit of truth can lead.

Already in one of his early dramas, *The Return of the Druses*, published in 1843, Browning wrestled with an inextricable problem of personality: the intricacies and complexities of good and evil conflicting in one nature. Browning was never interested in plain issues, doubtless because of the complexity of his own personality. Yet he thought himself simple. As G. K. Chesterton amusingly says:

He was . . . a man who loved above all things plain and sensational words, open catastrophes, a clear and ringing conclusion to everything. But it so happened, unfortunately, that his own words were not plain; that his catastrophes came with a crashing and sudden unintelligibleness which left men in doubt whether the thing were a catastrophe or a great stroke of good luck; that his conclusion, though it rang like a trumpet to the four corners of heaven, was in its actual message quite inaudible.[1]

This paradox of personality is common to many geniuses, and largely accounts for their disruptive influence in the affairs of ordinary life: they, so crystal-clear to themselves, are a source of confusion and often distress to their associates. Similarly, Browning never could understand the charge of obscurity brought against his work; his beautiful humility presupposed a world of Brownings; it never occurred to him that he possessed an outstanding intellect, a mind which functioned in an unusual manner, whereas the truth is that possibly no one except the one other human being fitted by nature to understand him—most happily, the woman he married—ever came within actual reach of the infinities of meaning in his work. Elizabeth Barrett understood inevitably, because her mind moved at a similar level, and derived from a similar source. But again, the " influence" of these two poets on each other's work was negligible: it is the perfect example of two minds from the beginning

[1] G. K. Chesterton, *Robert Browning*.

made for each other, each working in isolation and in ignorance of the other's existence towards the one moment in time when they at last met and instantly mingled, from which moment they reinforced, revitalized and strengthened each other, gave and received in perfect mental and spiritual unity, but never lost one fraction of their own individuality in the process. It was the "marriage of true minds" which, were life less imperfect, would be the rule rather than the exception. Perhaps if the ideal were held more tenaciously, and the imperfect less continuously accepted as inevitable, the old theory of the attraction of opposites might be superseded, and a new era in marriage begin. Certainly the prevailing belief has not led to outstandingly brilliant successes. The time has surely come for a fresh approach to the whole subject, essentially Christian, but not bound by Church dogma. The Church's view is founded on the assumption that every marriage approximates to the ideal; if indeed it were so, then marriage would be as indissoluble as the Church affirms. But in actual fact the very reverse is true, and the majority of marriages are contracted for anything but "ideal" reasons. This is largely due to the destruction through ill-advised interference of the earliest love-ideal. Young people are taught by cynical elders that the search for perfection must inevitably end in disillusionment and failure. Their earliest love-affair is treated with amusement. "The child's in love"; there is an element of humour in the realization, whereas in truth no experience in later life is nearer tragedy, because in youth love, and all other poignant experience, is known in isolation, divorced from the sense of significance or relation to life as a whole which can redeem the tragic problems of maturer years. The lovely youthful ideal is forced down into the unconscious, only to reappear years later, often with tragic results. But the day may come when the Browning marriage, rather than being cited as the happy exception to an unhappy rule, is regarded as the ideal to be sought, believed in through every vicissitude, and nothing less accepted. "Where there is no vision the people perish"; when ideals are discarded the soul shrivels, and life becomes a living death. Humanity will be saved only by the preservation of ideals. The "trailing clouds of glory" that enrich life need not "fade into the light of common day." There is no *common* day. Wordsworth wrote wisely of the child as the prophet. The child has a vision the years tragically obscure. Some years ago a novel apparently superficial but actually profound stressed in parable-form the cleavage between the child-world and the adult-world, and the reason for the cleavage.[1] It would be safe to say that all our troubles originate in a misunderstanding of sex.

[1] Christopher Morley, *Thunder on the Left.*

To sum up. Browning, as the great poet of humanity, fulfils all the demands for realism, ugliness and obscurity made by the modernists. In fact, Mr. DeVane in his recently published ***Browning Handbook*** remarks that in his own time

> Browning's manner was still too new, too familiar and racy, his utterance too broken.

It was the manner of the poetry of the future. In *Sordello* alone we find, even, indeed, in five lines, a baffling complexity of all three elements, which would be difficult to equal in contemporary poetry:

> "As knops that stud some almug to the pith
> Pricked for gum, wry thence, and crinkled worse
> Than pursed eye-lids of a river-horse
> Sunning himself o' the slime when whirrs the breeze"
> *Gad-fly*, that is. . . .

The obscurity of *Sordello* as a whole lies in the complexity of Browning's natural thought-method, which at that early period he had not the skill to simplify. As with many modern poets, his manner of expression unravelled with experience. *Sordello* was published when he was only twenty-eight, and is an epic achievement for so young a man. His thought runs on, in and out, to and fro, one image suggesting another till the main original theme is entangled in the threads and almost lost, travelling the world over, and even beyond the world, to the Mountains of the Moon, and all by way of an infinity of labyrinthine paths. It is difficult to see why this has ever been considered a dry or unreadable poem: the imagery is vivid and brilliant, the philosophy fine, the study of character and motive masterly; it contains exquisite love-poetry, and some of the loveliest nature-poetry Browning ever wrote. As an intellectual exercise it must surely be unparalleled. Here also are some of his best definitions of the poetic temperament:

> . . . A soul fit to receive
> Delight at every sense. . . .
>
> . . . .
>
> . . . exceeding love
> Becomes an aching weight. . . .
>
> . . . .
>
> . . . they fain invest
> The lifeless thing with life from their own souls.
>
> . . . .
>
> Visibly through his garden walketh God.
>
> . . . .
>
> Amid his wild-wood sig ts he lived alone
> As if the poppy felt with him.
>
> . . . .
>
> "How should externals satisfy my soul?"
>
> . . . .
>
> "What avail a poet's heart
> Verona's pomps and gauds? five blades of grass
> Suffice him. . . ."

And it is scarcely necessary to add that here again we come upon the passionate need to dig out the truth from the depths of a human soul. From first to last Browning's passion for humanity was the search for truth; this, in every human situation, every human character he explored, was his real goal.

> . . . Our human speech is naught;
> Our human testimony false, our fame
> And human estimation words and wind. . . .
>
> . . . .
>
> It is the glory and the good of Art
> That Art remains the one way possible
> Of speaking truth. . . .[1]

Nevertheless, he admits, a few lines further on, that the search is perilous:

> . . . here's the plague
> That all this trouble comes of telling truth.

We, reading *The Ring and the Book*, and hearing all sides, penetrate into the heart of the situation, which was naturally hidden from the actors in the drama, who were able to know only their own particular rôle. The author and the reader, however, become god-like in their ability to see the whole design, not only the fragments of the pattern. The major part of human

[1] *The Ring and the Book.*

suffering in a difficult situation lies in the incapacity to understand its true significance, see the whole, and relate the parts to it. So pain is experienced in isolation, instead of in an ultimately harmonious relation. On the reverse side of a piece of tapestry there is only a mass of tangled threads, conveying no meaning to the eye or the mind. But on the other side, hidden from us, is the perfectly woven picture, each thread forming an essential part of the design. In *Abt Vogler* Browning expresses a similar idea:

> On the earth the broken arcs; in the heaven a perfect
> round.

Life among short-sighted men can become almost unendurable to the man of vision, and it is possible that years of frustration produced at last *The Ring and the Book*, as the oyster's irritation produces the pearl. "Half-Rome" and "The Other Half-Rome" and "Tertium Quid" give the varying views of the ignorant world at large, all the worthless opinions of the onlookers who, knowing nothing, always claim to know everything. No wonder Caponsacchi cries in despair:

> Answer you, Sirs. Do I understand aright?
> Have patience! In this sudden smoke from hell,—
> So things disguise themselves,—I cannot see
> My own hand held thus broad before my face
> And know it again,

no wonder he groans:

> You must know that a man gets drunk with truth
> Stagnant inside him.

He knew too well how the judgments of the world would tarnish and belittle the exquisite truth. He gave his listeners a flower, knowing it must be muddied and torn in their rough fingers. Most of all he feared the resultant confusion in his own mind:

> So things disguise themselves, . . .

until

> . . . I cannot see
> My own hand held thus broad before my face.

This is the Iago-evil, the subtle power of insinuation that can, unless passionately resisted, destroy the highest values. Caponsacchi's ardent speech should suggest to the reader a fact commonly overlooked: that purity can be a passion, idealism a consuming fire.

> I have done with being judged.
> I stand here guiltless in thought, word and deed,
> To the point that I apprise you,—in contempt
> For all misapprehending ignorance
> O' the human heart, much more the mind of Christ,—
> That I assuredly did bow, was blessed
> By the revelation of Pompilia. There!
> Such is the final act I fling you, Sirs,
> To mouth and mumble and misinterpret: there!
> "The priest's in love," have it the vulgar way!

He ends in simple heart-broken pathos:

> Sirs, I am quiet again. You see, we are
> So very pitiable, she and I. . . .

A greater than he, wrongfully accused, and in danger of a malefactor's death, answered nothing:

> He answered him (Pilate) to never a word; insomuch that the governor marvelled greatly.

A greater, and a wiser; it is to be feared that all Caponsacchi's words were vain; degraded humanity chooses always to believe the scurrilous rather than the chaste, the trumpet of truth cannot sound in the ears of the wilfully deaf. So Caponsacchi grieves:

> . . . I thirst for truth
> But shall not drink it till I reach the source.

This, throughout his life, was Browning's own cry. "Shutting out fear with all the strength of hope" in poem after poem, drama after drama, he ceaselessly pursued the same elusive figure, forever veiled. Even in his second poem, *Paracelsus*, he realized the hopelessness of his quest:

> . . . You know my hopes;
> I am assured at length, those hopes were vain;
> That truth is just as far from me as ever.

Yet he had no choice but to continue. The whole theme of this poem, in fact is concerned with the philosopher's search for truth, and, in another form, *Sordello* continues the theme, the searcher this time a poet.

But ultimate truth, it seems, cannot be found; even if glimpsed, it cannot be told directly, only by parable or symbol. This fact is in itself perhaps a symbol of the half-life we live on earth.

CHAPTER II

THE POET OF LOVE

LOVE strikes the human consciousness as a risen sun lights the eye. . . . It is throned above all other knowledges that man's experience may know, bearing the crown and the sceptre to whose authority all human allegiance unhesitatingly bows. . . . It is life conscious of life, the highest pinnacle of life to which we come, and, being itself life's richest flower, holds the seeds of birth and of creation. In love man is more than human, or, if you will, then only attains humanity.[1]

This is pre-eminently Browning's view of love. He is England's greatest love-poet, for the reason that for him love is always an inclusive passion. Although he would have understood and appreciated *Epipsychidion* he would never have written such a poem himself. The tenuous, de-mortalized passion held no especial attraction for him. Browning was nothing if not human. With all its sorrows, frustrations, inadequacies and despairs, life on earth was for him a triumphant adventure, and although he pondered much on the life beyond death, he had no desire to hasten its coming, or to believe that imagined attributes of that life alone might be embodied satisfactorily in this life.

[1] G. Wilson Knight, *The Christian Renaissance.*

. . . All good things
Are ours, nor soul helps flesh more, now than flesh helps
soul.[1]

He never saw the body as a stumbling-block to spiritual progress, and love was equally a passion of body, soul, heart and mind. It would indeed be difficult to imagine a poet of his stature, vitality and virility accepting any other view. To some poets love comes lightly, they write of it in airy, flowing musical strains; love inspires, but with how volatile a breath; there are no profound depths to be troubled. To others, it comes as a spiritual exaltation, aspiring to realms where no breath of materialism tarnishes, as if through the enlightenment of one supreme experience the soul had learned to ride "naked on the air of heaven," but Browning wrote not only of essence but of "earth-attire" too, not only of "soul which makes all things new," but also of the "obvious human bliss," the "need to satisfy life's daily thirst with a thing men seldom miss."[2] That he clearly distinguishes between the concepts of mind and soul, thus disagreeing with many philosophers, is evident in stanzas VI and VII of *Charles Avison* (*Parleyings with Certain People of Importance in Their Day*). They are "distinct indisputably":

[1] *Rabbi Ben Ezra.*

[2] I have borrowed here and there in this chapter from my essay on *The Love-poetry of Robert Browning*, published some years ago, and now out of print.

. . . "So worked Mind, its tribe
Of sense ministrant above, below,
Far, near, or no or haply long ago
Brought to pass knowledge." But Soul's sea,—drawn
whence,
Fed how, forced whither,—by what evidence
Of ebb and flow, that's felt beneath the tread,
Soul has its course 'neath Mind's work overhead,—
Who tells of, tracks to source the founts of Soul.

The thought embodied in these lines is expanded in the two stanzas. The activities of the whole man are fourfold: the soul apprehends, the heart feels, the mind thinks, the body acts. Love, the most powerful of human emotions, must, in its perfection, include them all. "In its perfection." But perfection is rare; actually life usually compels the exclusion of one or several of these activities, and a passion which should be complete is forced to survive with one limb or more severed.

Browning's was supremely the poetry of transcendental humanism, written by a poet as healthfully whole as the writer of the greatest love-poem in the world, *The Song of Songs*. (If this be a poem not of human love but a symbolic presentation of the relation between Christ and the Church, it is unfortunate that such vividly erotic imagery should have been chosen, for while physical love is in itself essentially pure, its association with an altogether different type of emotion—different in kind, not degree—immediately debases both. There is a subtly unpleasant flavour about this magnificent poem unless it is interpreted as a work of transcendental humanism. As love-poetry, it is supreme; as mysticism, unwholesome. A fine line divides the sane from the unhealthy in mystical literature, for the very reason that the use of love-imagery is inevitable, yet the finest mystics and mystical poets avoid the pitfalls.) *The Song of Songs* is complete: despite the recurrent physical imagery there are repeated references to "him whom my soul loveth," no suggestion that this overmastering emotion is confined to the body alone. The flesh is irradiated with the passion of love, and in that exquisite blaze body and soul melt into one indivisible glory:

> Thy soul I know not from thy body,
> Nor thee from myself.

This was the love Browning believed in throughout his life, and this the love he found, which suggests that the ideal, passionately trusted, patiently awaited, must ultimately materialize. "Though the vision tarry, wait for it; because it will surely come."[1] When for Browning it came, there was no choice: this he must have known from the outset, although throughout there would be an illusion of choice. It happened that the following of the vision meant overthrowing his one consuming moral passion: the passion for truth. He,

[1] *Habbakuk* ii. 3.

the living embodiment of truth, the great poet of truth, the Christian seeing in truth his God, was compelled to accept all the horrors of deception, to live for sixteen interminable months a life of dishonesty, to compromise daily with his soul, endure, during those months glowing with the wonder of the ideal found at last, what can have been for him nothing less than hell. Is it not conceivable that he, pre-eminently the poet of dramatic situations and spiritual conflicts, was by nature predestined to precisely this type of problem in his own life? There is a profound justice in the theory that every man is given the type of experience he understands. Yet there was really no choice: the final issue was implicit in the beginning. And soon it was clear that once again, through the torturing thickets of deception, he was fighting his way in the cause of truth. Elizabeth Barrett's father stood for false values, and for that reason, if for no other, he must be vanquished. Personal ties, filial duty, the claims and loyalties of the family, all so momentous in Victorian days, must be sacrificed to the greater good. Throughout the conflict he fought for truth, life and freedom as much as for love, and was tried almost to the limit of his strength. Justice was more to him than any personal issue. Had he been able to detach himself from the situation and view it objectively, it would have provided material for the greatest of his dramas, a complex drama after his own heart. But the great poet shrinks from autobiography: the personal problem may appear and re-appear in his work in a hundred transmuted forms; the actual drama of his own life must not be directly portrayed. This accounts for Browning's excessive sensitivity about *Pauline;* Matthew Arnold's acute criticism of the poem as autobiography caused him to plunge into the dramatic art-form, speaking henceforward only through the mouths of others, some imaginary, some historical. G. K. Chesterton in his study of Browning suggests that the situation in which Caponsacchi found himself echoes much of Browning's own conflict more than twelve years earlier, but it is never really safe to isolate a poet's experience in relation to his work. So much, or so little, may go to the making of a poem. The circumstances of the priest's difficulty in *The Ring and the Book* have little actual affinity with Browning's own; the similarity lies in the fact that in both cases emotional and moral values were pre-eminently at issue. And both Caponsacchi and Browning sacrificed the lesser, which was apparently the greater, for the truly greater good. There are times when even high moral concepts must be overridden. In both these instances the life of a human being was at stake, the life of a human soul. Caponsacchi dared not leave Pompilia to perdition, nor could Browning consent to what would have been the virtual murder of Elizabeth

Barrett, for had he not rescued her, death would soon have overtaken her. He was her saviour, and he knew it, and had the courage to accept all that the knowledge involved. This knowledge, among innumerable other factors, included the realization that the mental and physical stress of the situation might equally bring about her end. The "romance" of the Browning love-story has been dwelt upon often; a playwright has made of it a successful play, but only a Browning himself, or a Shakespeare, could write the drama it actually was.

Browning has been called the poet of vital moments; Chesterton speaks of his "doctrine of the great hour." Some of the lines in *Cristina*, published three years before Browning and Elizabeth Barrett met, foreshadowed the vital moment, the great hour, in Browning's own life:

> Oh, we're sunk enough here, God knows!
> But not quite so sunk that moments,
> Sure though seldom, are denied us,
> When the spirit's true endowments
> Stand out plainly from its false ones,
> And apprise it if pursuing
> Or the right way or the wrong way
> To its triumph or undoing.
>
> . . . .
>
> Doubt you if, in some such moment,
> As she fixed me, she felt clearly,
> Ages past the soul existed,

Here an age, 'tis resting merely,
And hence fleets again for ages,
While the true end, sole and single,
It stops here for is, this love-way,
With some other soul to mingle.

. . . .

Doubt you whether
This she felt as, looking at me,
Mine and her souls rushed together?

For Browning the subsequent fulfilment was, happily, complete, not only the spiritual one experienced by the lover in the poem. He was spared the reflection:

She has lost me, I have gained her;
Her soul's mine, and thus, grown perfect,
I shall pass my life's remainder.
Life will just hold out the proving
Both our powers, *alone* [1] and blended. . . .

for his powers were merged at last with the powers of the woman he loved, and there was no need to cry: "then, come the next life quickly," they found fulfilment here and now. This was their reward for sacrificing many apparent virtues. There are circumstances in which the great man—whose life is not his own, for the genius belongs to the world, not to himself, or to any human being—must submit to no recognized law, but must accept the titanic responsibility of being a aw to himself.

[1] The italics are mine.

Many of Browning's poems are concerned with the tragedy of loves that miss the desired end—clearly through some fault or weakness in the lovers. Foremost among them is the famous poem *The Statue and the Bust*, where the whole complicated problem of accepted morality versus the true good is wrestled with:

> The sin I impute to each frustrate ghost
> Is, the unlit lamp and the ungirt loin,
> Though the end in sight was a vice, I say.

The lovers, the bride of the Riccardi and the Duke Ferdinand, loved at first sight:

> He looked at her, as a lover can;
> She looked at him, as one who awakes:
> The past was a sleep, and her life began.

At last she decided:

> I fly to the Duke who loves me well,
>
> . . . .
>
> And I save my soul—but not to-morrow. . . .
>
> . . . .
>
> Is one day more so long to wait?

"But not to-morrow," and so, for various reasons, action was delayed, until:

> . . . Weeks grew months, years; gleam by gleam
> The glory dropped from their youth and love,
> And both perceived they had dreamed a dream. . . .
>
> . . . .

I hear you reproach, "But delay was best,
For their end was a crime"—oh, a crime will do
As well, I reply, to serve for a test,
As a virtue golden through and through.

Clearly it seemed no crime to the lady to remain with her husband, though her heart cried:

If I spend the night with that devil twice,
May his window serve as my loop for hell
Where a damned soul looks on Paradise!

The estate of matrimony is holy, no matter what the circumstances; she remained virtuous; there is no technical sin in surrendering the body to one man while mind and heart live with another. They avoided the vice of adultery; it remains for God to judge whether physical sin is more grave than a spiritual crime.

Again, in the short, apparently simple, even, it might seem, trifling, poem *Youth and Art*, a similar disaster is portrayed:

It once might have been, once only . . .

The chance comes only once, but

. . . we missed it, lost it for ever,

with the result that

Each life's unfulfilled, you see;
It hangs still, patchy and scrappy:
We have not sighed deep, laughed free,
Starved, feasted, despaired, been happy.

The girl becomes a famous singer, the boy a Royal Academician, but these honours are no compensation for the fullness of life they lost because he "would not be rash," she "rasher and something over." Again and again Browning reiterates this disaster: in *Dis Aliter Visum*;[1] in *Inapprehensiveness*, *Too Late*, *Bifurcation*, and it is noteworthy that his particular preoccupation with the subject came after the joy he had himself found through not allowing the vital moment to elude him. In so far as it is ever possible to dogmatize about a poet's personal views, it is safe to affirm that he believed—romantically, perhaps, it might be thought, with an irrational idealism—in the validity of one supreme love-experience for every human being, the chance that comes once, once only, and that since the attainment of fullest life is finally the one duty, to ignore or refuse this opportunity is a sin. Again, if the love-ideal were trusted, if it were not derided and debased until it becomes no more than a romantic fiction to be regarded with suspicion and embarrassment, most of the tragedies of love would be

[1] Mr. DeVane in the *Browning Handbook* has an interesting note on the sub-title of this poem: "Le Byron de nos jours." He says: Possibly the title is ironic, and Browning means to point the difference between the dashing Byron who never failed to assert his love when he felt it, and the over-cautious lover of the poem. Possibly Browning has in mind Byron's poem *The Dream*, where he protests to Mary Chaworth that his life and hers would not have been ruined if she had accepted his love when he had offered it years before.

averted. And it is not an exaggeration to assert that almost every human tragedy, traced to its source, is a tragedy of love.

The woman in the poem *Bifurcation*, having chosen duty—clearly her plain duty: "My reason bade prefer duty to love"—had really no choice but to console herself with the thoughts that have provided consolation, even if cold, for thousands of women trapped by similar circumstances:

> But deep within my heart of hearts there hid
> Ever the confidence, amends for all,
> That heaven repairs what wrong earth's journey did
> When love from life-long exile comes at call.
> Duty and love, one broadway, were the best—
> Who doubts? But one or other was to choose.
> I chose the darkling half, and wait the rest
> In that new world where light and darkness fuse.

Nevertheless, it is conceivable that the choice of darkling duty may be the wrong choice. It is possible that a clearer understanding of the duty of living a life of joy, blessedness and fulfilment rather than enduring a colourless acceptance of the doctrine of frustration might accelerate the coming of the Kingdom of Heaven. But the truth is buried very deep: failure and error are really due to an incomplete understanding of the laws governing life. This poem has a quality of grey resignation very different from some of the earlier love-poems of triumph in failure.

In *Inapprehensiveness* we share the actual moment of lost opportunity:

By you stands, and may
So stand, unnoticed to the Judgment Day,
One who, if once aware that your regard
Claimed what his heart holds—woke, as from its sward
The flower, the dormant passion, would startling wreak
Revenge on your inapprehensive stare. . . .
You let your eyes meet mine, touch what you term
Quietude, that's an universe in germ—
The dormant passion needing but a look
To burst into immense life.

But she baffles him by speaking calmly of a book which, she says, is not by Ruskin.

Although Browning believed passionately in the ideal of the "love that greatens and glorifies," his wide knowledge of life would not allow him to ignore the problems of unrequited love, tragic inequalities in the lovers' capacity for loving, or danger latent in the trivial too easily grown gigantic, as in *A Lover's Quarrel:*

See a word, how it severeth!
Oh, power of life and death
In the tongue. . . .

. . . . . .

Woman, and will you cast
For a word, quite off at last
Me, your own, your You—
Since, as truth is true

> I was You all the happy past—
> Me do you leave aghast
> With the memories we amassed?

and again in *A Woman's Last Word:*

> What so wild as words are?

But these are the quarrels of the lesser lovers; great love survives, nor indeed can ever know, the petty misunderstandings, the bitter words that wound and sever. In *A Lover's Quarrel* the man was mistaken in looking to her "for the pure and true, and the beauteous and the right." Had she possessed these qualities, she would not have "cast him off for a word." "Love suffereth long, *and is kind*." Although it may be argued that the love here referred to is the divine emotion for which we have no exact word and which, to avoid confusion, is sometimes translated as "charity," yet the love known as human can be neither true nor great unless it fulfils in every detail St. Paul's definition in I *Corinthians* xiii., and "beareth all things, believeth all things, hopeth all things, endureth all things."

In Browning's love-poetry it is invariably the man who understands the triumph of the mysterious self-fulfilment of love: the truth that no great love is ever lost, that in the emotion itself, by virtue of its enriching and deepening effects in the lover's nature, is the true, possibly in the last resort the truest, fulfilment. The lover experiences in himself such heights, depths and riches that no actual consummation can really add to the miracle. This philosophy is perhaps best expressed in *The Last Ride Together*, when the man, despite his failure, since "nothing all his love avails, since all his life seemed meant for, fails" can still say:

> My whole heart rises up to bless
> Your name in pride and thankfulness.

He is blessed in his own capacity for love, and in the memory of his happy hopes. Only he himself can destroy that treasure. His state, after all, is far happier than that of the lover in *Two in the Campagna*, who is tormented with an insatiable longing:

> I would that you were all to me,
> You that are just so much, no more. . . .
>
> . . . .
>
> Where does the fault lie? What the core
> Of the wound, since wound must be?

This poem reflects one of the most delicate and profound tragedies of love: there is no "fault," no core that can be rooted out and destroyed; it is the subtle tragedy of inequality in loving, the rather common tragedy of the sacrifice of the greater for the lesser; no one is to blame, it is simply that she lacks the capacity to love in the same degree as he. Possibly the love is actually different in kind. Certainly it is the antithesis of the emotion in *One Word More*, *By the Fireside*, in the last lines of *Prospice*, in the words from *The Ring and the Book:*

> O lyric love; half angel and half bird,
> And all a wonder, and a wild desire. . . .

in stanza IX of *Any Wife to any Husband:*

> But now, because the hour through years was fixed
> Because our inmost beings met and mixed,
> Because thou once hast loved me—wilt thou dare
> Say to the soul and Who may list beside,
> "Therefore she is immortally my bride;
> Chance cannot change my love, nor time impair."

If chance cannot change love, nor time impair, time is conquered; all the vicissitudes of life, the undermining possibilities that are the torment and despair of every lover, have no power. The profound conviction of the great lover, wherein he becomes akin to the mystic: that the emotion of love itself transcends the lovers, is his final consolation even in bitterest betrayal or loss. In their interesting and provocative book *The Voyage to Illyria*, the authors seek to prove that Shakespeare overcame in this way the agony of betrayal he suffered in his own life, and embodied his creed in the metaphysical poem *The Phœnix and the Turtle*. Love is for every poet a metaphysical problem, and the way from Inferno to Paradise is only through the gateway of a transcendental faith in love itself. And the true divinity of love is demonstrated by the fact that every great work of art, almost every spiritual experience, every way to God, is through the Eros. Hence the debasement of love is the worst blasphemy, the unforgivable sin; small wonder that it is punished as no other crime, that the punishment falls not only on the sinner but persists "unto the third and fourth generation." Human love is the greatest of God's gifts, through which every man can attain divinity, but "that which leads to the stars can lead to the abyss"[1]; it remains always with the individual to decide the direction. But here again, the derision of which the developing child so often becomes aware on first feeling the impact of the love-consciousness is directly responsible for the loss of faith, and once faith is lost, the descent is rapid. To love is greater than to be loved, for the reason, known to every mystic, every philosopher, and plainly declared by Jesus, that the true life is within, and can neither be decreased nor increased by actual outward events. "Not that which goeth in . . . but that which cometh out." The material is received from without, but the work on the material is done within, and it remains with the individual to create from it beauty or ugliness, good or evil. The world, looking always and only for

[1] Fiona Macleod, *The Distant Country.*

obvious results, derides the reality or worth of spiritual fulfilment; the labour often becomes too arduous for the lover, who finds the worldly pressure, allied to his own natural desire for actual fulfilment, too strong, and he succumbs to despair. But despair is no practical solution to a problem. In this circumstance, again, the spiritual man is really the practical man: he has a solution where the materialist has none.

For Browning, the practical idealist, there never was a cleavage between body and spirit; he knew the conflict between body, soul and mind to be fundamentally false, knew how to find peace in a fusion of a trinity too often at war. In *By the Fireside*, the poem of a perfect marriage, the husband looks back over the happy years, and recalls the moment in the woods among the hills where

> The lights and shades made up a spell
> Till the trouble grew and stirred,

and she "filled his empty heart at a word," they "were mixed at last, in spite of the mortal screen." He muses happily on their unity:

> When, if I think but deep enough,
> You are wont to answer, prompt as rhyme,
> And you, too, find without a rebuff,
> The response your soul seeks many a time,
> Piercing its fine flesh-stuff.

This is the marriage of true minds:

> Oh, I must feel your brain prompt mine,
> Your heart anticipate my heart,
> You must be just before, in fine,
> See, and make me see, for your part,
> New depths of the Divine,

the converse of the experience portrayed in *Two in the Campagna.*

Browning can portray aspects of love as cruel as the emotions of the thwarted woman in *The Laboratory*, who desires a subtle poison to kill her rival, and the bitter feelings of the ageing queen in *In a Balcony* when she finds the man she loves in the arms of young and lovely Constance:

> Too late—no love for you, too late for love. . . .
> See, I am old—look here, you happy girl,
> I will not play the fool, deceive myself,
> 'Tis all gone, put your cheek beside my cheek,
> Ah! what a contrast does the moon behold!

The obvious tragedies of love, as contrasted with the hidden dramas, are depicted in *In a Gondola*, in *Too Late*, the cry of the man who "loved the woman so well who married the other," and in *Porphyria's Lover*. This last poem may be viewed from many angles, and its significance interpreted in various ways, but the picture of the lover winding Porphyria's hair "three times her little throat around" haunts the mind as curiously repellent, because of the psychological abnormality of the whole poem. The references to hair in *Porphyria's Lover* and in *In a Gondola* are noteworthy; in *Porphyria* she "let the damp hair fall," "and all her yellow hair displaced," "and spread o'er all her yellow hair," finally:

> All her hair I wound
> Three times her little throat around;

he strangled her with her yellow hair. And in *In a Gondola* the lover when he is dying cries:

> . . . care
> Only to put aside thy beauteous hair
> My blood will hurt!

Even at the moment of death he thinks of her lovely hair. *Porphyria's Lover* has throughout an affinity with the closing thought of *In a Gondola:* death is greeted as a friend at the moment of supreme fulfilment, for to continue to live would be too difficult. Life after a transcendent experience is always dangerous: day by day there is fear of assault on the once-realized, and since jealously guarded, ideal. If Othello had died when he cried:

> . . . If it were now to die,
> 'Twere now to be most happy,

the subsequent greater tragedy would have been averted. It may be for this reason that the concept of perfection and death is constant throughout poetry: the two are inextricably linked in the human mind. Antony and Cleopatra seek the final consummation of their love in death.[1] Dante finds perfection only after the death of Beatrice; a similar thought is expressed in Keats's last sonnet, often in Shelley, and it occurs frequently in Browning, as when in *In a Balcony* Norbert says: "This must end here; it is too perfect." This recalls Othello's:

> . . . I fear
> My soul hath her content so absolute
> That not another comfort like to this
> Succeeds in unknown fate. . . .
> . . . . . .
> . . . it is too much of joy.

Browning's first poem *Pauline* is concerned largely with love and death. Recently in his novel *Sparkenbroke* Mr. Charles Morgan writes of the poet's conception of death as "life's high meed," and of the inevitable link between love-consummation and death. There is a deep-rooted conviction that life cannot embrace the perfect; or that after having once touched those heights the continuance of life is certain to cause a plunge into the abyss of despair, or some form of death-in-life, and actual death is preferred. This is

[1] Cf. "The Transcendental Humanism of Antony and Cleopatra" in *The Imperial Theme*, by G. Wilson Knight.

possibly in essence a theological conception, allied to the doctrine of the Fall. Certainly the theory subsumes a profound lack of faith, a denial of any belief in the divinity of life on earth. A more positive attitude might prove a shorter way to the Kingdom of Heaven. To equate love with life rather than with death must be God's will for man, since God is Himself love, and so long as life's imperfections and frustrations are accepted as inevitable, most of all by the poets, who are the true prophets and leaders, we shall continue to grope blindfolded through a thorny wilderness. We need more faith in life itself.

It is significant that the consummation the lovers experience and long for death to perpetuate is always the transcendental consummation; there is no dread of loss in physical fulfilment, naturally, perhaps, since normally physical union creates life. But the deeper union should, and must, if we are to redeem human life, be creative too. It must not lead to death. It should be possible to incarnate the transcendental. Again, the conception of a cleavage between matter and spirit is too generally accepted.

In *Porphyria's Lover* it seems clear that the lover dreads physical fulfilment, that he cannot face the knowledge that the consummate moment he experiences when he reflects:

> . . . At last I knew
> Porphyria worshipped me,

must pass, losing its perfection in a human fulfilment which, to his understanding, must by comparison seem subtly debased.

> . . . Surprise
> Made my heart swell, and still it grew
> While I debated what to do.

Then death is deliberately chosen.

> . . . No pain felt she
> I am quite sure she felt no pain. . . .

and so through the night they sit together, the moment made eternal by death, and approved, so the lover feels, by God, Who "has not said a word."

In *Evelyn Hope* there is a belief, as in *Bifurcation*, that the love unfulfilled on earth will be complete after death. Theosophists have taken this poem, and the poem *Cristina*, as evidence of Browning's belief in reincarnation, but the last word on the subject of his philosophy is surely that he was a full-blooded, whole-hearted Christian, and so would sympathetically consider the innumerable divergent theories on life and immortality while himself maintaining throughout an aloof, non-committal attitude in essence profoundly Christlike. The truth is neither here nor there, only echoes resound in the various jarring sects. It is not possible to isolate the "philosophy of Jesus Christ," and for the active Christian the many theories pale beside the vital belief in God Himself, and the revelation of God in Christ. Browning was nothing if not a "liberal Christian."

Too Late is also concerned with death:

> But, dead! All's done with: wait who may,
> Watch and wear and wonder who will,
> Oh, my whole life that ends to-day!
> Oh, my soul's sentence, sounding still,
> "The woman is dead, that was none of his;
> And the man, that was none of hers, may go!"
> There's only the last left: worry that!

In the following lines the poet of romantic love plunges into realism as brutal as any poetry written to-day:

> Wreak, like a bull, on the empty coat,
> Rage, its late wearer is laughing at!
> Tear the collar to rags, having missed his throat;
> Strike stupidly on—"This, this and this,
> Where I would that a bosom received the blow!"

Remorse at his lost opportunities consumes the speaker; again Browning returns to the theme of the one chance missed:

> I ought to have done more. . . .
> . . . .
> . . . borne you away to a rock for us two,

now, too late, he mourns: "If only it would come over again!" this neglected opportunity. But she is dead:

> . . . You cannot speak
> From the churchyard neither, miles removed,

Though I feel by a pulse within my cheek,
Which stabs and stops, that the woman I loved
Needs help in her grave, and finds none near. . . .

He, like the lovers in *Youth and Art*, has "missed it, lost it forever," nor has he known the spiritual fulfilment of the lover in *Cristina*, who can cry triumphantly "she has lost me, I have gained her." In *Too Late* there is a description of the woman which in its bare colloquialism has a very modern ring:

And your mouth—there was never, to my mind,
Such a funny mouth, for it would not shut;
And the dented chin, too—what a chin!
There were certain ways when you spoke, some words
That you knew you never could pronounce:
You were thin, however; like a bird's
Your hand seemed—some would say, the pounce
Of a scaly-footed hawk—all but!
The world was right when it called you thin.

Conversely, the triumphant poem of love and death is *Prospice:*

For sudden the worst turns the best to the brave,
The black minute's at end,
And the elements' rage, the fiend-voices that rave,
Shall dwindle, shall blend,
Shall change, shall become first a peace out of pain
Then a light, then thy breast,
O thou soul of my soul! I shall clasp thee again,
And with God be the rest!

By the time this was published (in the volume

Dramatis Personæ, 1864) Browning's faith in the conquest of death by love had been tested and not found wanting; he had no doubt that "death is the keeper of unknown redemptions"[1] and knew that human love at its highest, the love he had believed in and found, could not be bounded by the short span of earthly life. A belief in immortality is indeed integral to a faith in love as a supreme value; the love-experience in itself an intimation of immortality, evidenced in the sense of timelessness and sudden awakening to eternal values and the necessity for them. Here, again, Eros is the messenger of God.

Pauline, although written when Browning was only twenty, is an extraordinarily beautiful poem of love, foreshadowing, among all the other attributes of his future development, his consistent view of love as "the only good in the world," embodying the high ideal he never consented to lower. He could write as idealistically of love at seventy as at twenty; in fact, he was seventy-five or six, and nearing his death, when he wrote the passionate love-poem *Now* in *Asolando:*

Thought and feeling and soul and sense
Merged in a moment which gives me at last
You around me for once,
You beneath me, above me—
Me—sure that despite of time future, time past—
This tick of our life-time's one moment you love me.

[1] Fiona Macleod.

It remains to be proved whether the quintessence of love be not independent of sexual passion, and therefore conqueror of the years.

In the poet the romantic consciousness can never fade, though it will develop and deepen as youth grows to middle age, and maturity grows at last to old age. To-day psychologists who were once content to accept the purely materialistic explanation of the art-impulse are compelled to admit an element in it that defies analysis. Human life is not so simple that its profoundest and highest impulses can be reduced to scientific formulæ. Professor Hywel Hughes in his valuable book *The Philosophic Basis of Mysticism* explores the various theories concerning the mystic, and proves conclusively that true mysticism has no connection with physical abnormality, as many psycho-analysts have been at pains to prove. As William James points out,[1] the test of all such experiences is in their fruits; if the fruits be sound and of lasting benefit to mankind, the generating experience cannot have been "abnormal." One day we may come to realize that the spiritual man is the normal man, and that spiritual experience, the gift of prophecy, inspiration, and kindred qualities, should not be looked upon with suspicion and a degree of fear, since this really implies a low estimate of man's destiny, and no belief in the willingness of God to reveal Himself through

[1] *The Varieties of Religious Experience.*

humanity. The theory that St. Paul's vision on the road to Damascus was in actuality an epileptic seizure may be interesting to medical science, but it has little real value, since it cannot account for the subsequent results of the experience, nor detract from their enduring and far-reaching worth. There is a desirable *via media* between blind emotional belief and cold intellectual mistrust, and a rational, sympathetic approach to the supernormal has become an urgent necessity. Freud, among many discoveries of incalculable value to mental science, has perhaps done most good in proving, by theories evolved to prove the exact opposite, the impossibility and absurdity of reducing all human passion and aspiration to terms of sex. In a similar way, the materialist philosophers have defeated their own ends. It will be interesting to watch the results of the inevitable reaction from these one-sided views.

So the love that time cannot impair, the impulse that drives the poet's pen, defies the psycho-analysts, and enables Browning to write as romantically of love in old age as in youth. There is love-poetry in *Ferishtah's Fancies*, published five years before he died, as beautiful and vivid as any in the *Dramatic Lyrics* of forty years earlier. And the exquisite short lyric *Never the Time and the Place* appeared in the volume *Jocaseria* in 1883. There is an echo in this poem of *A Lover's Quarrel* written so long before:

Outside are the storms and the strangers; we
Oh, close, safe, warm, sleep I and she,
—I and she!—*Never the Time and the Place.*

Dearest, three months ago!
When we lived blocked-up with snow—
When the wind would edge
In and in his wedge,
In, in as far as the point would go—
Not to our ingle, though,
Where we loved each the other so.
—*A Lover's Quarrel.*

And in both poems there are lovely descriptions of spring, in the world, and in the lover's heart.

None of Browning's love-poetry can be called simple, although *A Woman's Last Word*, *In a Year*, *The Lost Mistress*, *Meeting at Night*, *Parting at Morning*, *Garden Fancies*, *Love in a Life*, *Life in a Love*, give an illusion of simplicity.

Love in a Life, in spite of its brevity and its artless diction, is a poignant parable of the search for love:

Room after room
I hunt the house through
We inhabit together.
Heart, fear nothing, heart, thou shalt find her—
Next time, herself! . . .

. . . .

Yet the day wears,
And door succeeds door;
I try the fresh fortune—

Range the wide house from the wing to the centre.
Still the same chance! she goes out as I enter. . . .

In *Life in a Love* he questions:

My life is a fault at last, I fear:
It seems too much like a fate, indeed!

But the indomitable philosophy of courage prevails:

But what if I fail of my purpose here?
It is but to keep the nerves at strain,
To dry one's eyes and laugh at a fall
And baffled, get up and begin again—
So the chase takes up one's life, that's all. . . .
. . . .

No sooner the old hope goes to ground
Than a new one, straight to the self-same mark,
I shape me—
Ever
Removed!

The ideal will not be abandoned. It cannot be at fault; in some way the search is faulty, not the goal unattainable, and the ideal remains throughout inviolate, as in *One Way of Love*, when the lover reflects:

My whole life long I learned to love.
This hour my utmost art I prove
And speak my passion—heaven or hell?
She will not give me heaven? 'Tis well!
Lose who may—I still can say,
Those who win heaven, blest are they.

Throughout Browning's love-poetry runs the unfailing belief in the glory of loving, in the enrichment through the love-experience itself:

> I said—Then dearest, since 'tis so,
> Since now at length my fate I know,
> Since nothing all my love avails,
> Since all my life seemed meant for, fails,
> Since this was written, and needs must be—
> My whole heart rises up to bless
> Your name in pride and thankfulness. . . .[1]

The lover, through the wisdom gained by his emotion, has grown to a spiritual stature which enables him to philosophize profoundly about his own disaster. "To the understanding, defeat is no less interesting than victory." It occurs to him also that even if life had granted him the love-fulfilment he desired, "still one must lead some life beyond." Life is greater even than love. Yet his intuition of love's immortality is evidenced in the last stanza:

> . . . .
>
> What if heaven be that, fair and strong
> At life's best, with our eyes upturned
> Whither life's flower is first discerned,
> We, fixed so, ever should so abide?
>
> . . . .
>
> Changed not in kind but in degree,
> The instant made eternity?

[1] *The Last Ride Together.*

A Woman's Last Word is almost an error in taste; here the poet seems to trespass. The ground is too intimate, or his manner of approach a trifle indiscreet. The extreme simplicity of diction tends to belittle the content. The poem might have been less embarrassingly personal if it had been written ten years later, although possibly the maturer Browning would then not have written it at all. The simplicity trembles on the verge of weakness, especially in the last stanza. It is an instance, rare in Browning, where the reader feels he has been intruding on privacies that should not be revealed to an outsider. The fault, of course, must lie in the manner, not the matter, of the poem. Art is normally concerned with deep intimacies. G. K. Chesterton is right in saying:

> I am not prepared to admit that there is or can be, properly speaking, in the world anything that is too sacred to be known. Whenever, therefore, a poet or any similar type of man can, or conceives that he can, make all men partakers in some splendid secret of his own heart, I can imagine nothing saner and nothing manlier than his course in doing so. . . . But the one essential . . . is that the man believes that he can make the story as stately to the whole world as it is to him, and he chooses his words to that end.[1]

If he fails, the sacredness of the experience is violated, and it is this violation that shocks us in *A Woman's*

[1] *Robert Browning.*

Last Word. Browning has written often of the intimacies of marriage, notably, and most successfully, in Pompilia's narrative in *The Ring and the Book*, and here no sense of intrusion is roused in the reader. The innocent child, trapped into a cruel marriage, when she feels

> . . . there was just one thing Guido claimed
> I had no right to give nor he to take,
> *We being in estrangement, soul from soul,*[1]

goes to her Church, to the Archbishop indeed, for guidance, but he, true to the Church's doctrines, upholds the "sanctity" of this vile marriage, commands her to "go home, embrace your husband quick." No circumstance, however foul, not even her confession that her brother-in-law, a priest, makes amorous advances to her at which her husband connives, can invalidate the sacrament. She must live with her husband, although her whole soul trembles with the intuition that such mating is blasphemy. She protests:

> There my husband never used deceit.
> He never did by speech nor act imply
> "Because of our soul's yearning that we meet
> And mix in soul through flesh, which yours and mine
> Wear and impress, and make their visible selves,—
> All of which means, for the love of you and me,
> Let us become one flesh, being one soul."

But the Archbishop sends her back to her despair:

[1] The italics are mine.

So, home I did go; so, the worst befell:
So, I had proof the Archbishop was just man,
And hardly that, and certainly no more,

(she had felt assured he "stood for God")

. . . .

. . . henceforth I looked to God
Only, nor cared my desecrated soul
Should have gay walls, gay windows for the world.

. . . .

Henceforth I asked God counsel, not mankind.

But because this union bears the name of marriage, the holy estate, honourable among all men, and is ratified by the Church, it must be endured, even it is commended. The conditions of its institution, the degradations of the subsequent relationship, are of no account. The estate of matrimony is sacramental. Similarly, the passionately sacred love for Caponsacchi that later comes to bless and save her is "unlawful," and therefore to be condemned by the Church, and by the world. In vain she may cry:

The glory of his nature, I had thought,
Shot itself out in white light, blazed the truth
Through every atom of his act with me. . . .

she sees clearly:

Yet where I point you, through the crystal shrine,
Purity in quintessence, one dew-drop,
You all descry a spider in the midst.

B.

In vain. The judgments of the Church and the world are rigid. Marriage is sanctified; all love outside marriage unhallowed. God may have joined together those who have not stood together at the altar, and remained absent from a ceremony essentially secular although performed in a church, but to allow flexible thinking on so dangerous a subject would lead to moral confusion, so the only safe course is to endorse the law. The truth, however, is that sincere Christian thought and teaching would avert such disasters. There would be no moral confusion if marriage were approached with Christian understanding and reverence. There may be a dangerous transition-period while the hard law as it stands is overthrown, and a certain amount of harm may be done in the name of freedom, as almost inevitably happens during a period of revolution, but there can be no true morality, no true spiritual freedom, until this most vital of human problems is approached from a new, creatively Christian angle.

The story of the love of Pompilia and Caponsacchi marks the peak of Browning's achievement in love-poetry. In this, his greatest work, the passion for truth and for love carry him to the heights. Pompilia cries:

> Therefore, because this man restored my soul
> All has been right.

God's law of the soul's salvation may not be man's

law. The love God has ordained may not necessarily be the love the world approves. This is for each soul alone, and for God, to judge. Pompilia judged, and knew:

> I did pray, do pray, in the prayer shall die,
> "Oh, to have Caponsacchi for my guide!"
> Ever the face upturned to mine, the hand
> Holding my hand across the world—a sense
> That reads, as only such can read, the mark
> God sets on woman, signifying so
> She should,—shall peradventure—be divine. . . .

By her love for Caponsacchi she is not only saved from the desecration and degradation of her marriage, she is forever deified. Although the Church failed her and drove her back to her despair, she could not lose her faith in God; though she was "miserable three drear years" she still trusted in

> . . . God the strong, God the beneficent,
> God, ever mindful in all strife and strait,
> Who, for our own good, makes the need extreme,
> Till at the last He puts forth might and saves.

At last the star rose, and Caponsacchi, whom men called sinner, drew her up into the light.

> . . . Say, from the deed, no touch
> Of harm came, but all good, all happiness,
> Not one faint speck of failure. . . .

Pompilia, dying, with her last breath proclaims the divinity of her passion:

Do not the dead wear flowers when dressed for God?
Say—I am all in flowers from head to foot!
. . . Not one flower of all he said and did,
Might seem to flit unnoticed, fade unknown,
But dropped a seed, has grown a balsam-tree
Whereof the blossoming perfumes the place
At this supreme of moments!

Then, so nearly purged of life, her thoughts already tinged with the clarity of eternity, she reflects on the mysteries of human love, human marriage:

> Marriage on earth seems such a counterfeit,
> Mere imitation of the inimitable:
> In heaven we have the real and true and sure.
> 'Tis there they neither marry nor are given
> In marriage; but are as the angels: right,
> Oh how right that is, how like Jesus Christ
> To say that! Marriage-making for the earth. . . .
>
> . . . .
>
> Be as the angels rather, who, apart,
> Know themselves into one, are found at length
> Married, but marry never, no, nor give
> In marriage: they are man and wife at once
> When the true time is. . . .

She and Caponsacchi are already united in that heavenly marriage; again, death will fulfil what life has denied. "Marriage on earth seems such a counterfeit" compared with this true marriage of mind and soul. This, not necessarily the legal wedlock, is the joining together that may not be sundered by man.

To descend from the heights of love immortalized in *The Ring and the Book* to the lesser passion reflected in *The Lost Mistress*, *In a Year*, and *Meeting at Night, Parting at Morning*, is not easy, but Browning was too great a poet to convey certain aspects of life only: his concern was with all types of humanity and human emotion, not only with the lovers capable of the heights and the depths, but also with those who suffer only for trivial causes, yet to the limit of their capacity. The girl in *In a Year*, wondering perplexedly:

> Was it something said,
> Something done,
> Vexed him? was it touch of hand,
> Turn of head?
> Strange! that very way
> Love begun:
> I as little understand
> Love's decay,

could not know that the emotion she called love was as far from the sacred passion of Pompilia and Caponsacchi as earth from the remotest star. So small a thing as "something said, something done" could not have shaken them; their love, rooted in eternity, God-given and ordained, and given by them back to God in reverence and thankfulness, would not suffer the torments of the lovers who, in professing to love each other, are really only loving themselves, and are therefore ready to take offence and break the relationship at every least hint of misunderstanding. False love is built on pride, true love on humility, and the depths of human affection make of every man and woman a Christian.

The Lost Mistress conveys briefly in five four-line stanzas the pain of friendship only when love is desired:

> Yet I will but say what mere friends say,
> Or only a thought stronger;
> I will hold your hand but so long as all may,
> Or so very little longer.

But deep love will wait for ever, in cool, undemanding friendship if need be, if the beloved, and the ideal of love, is served thereby.

Meeting at Night, *Parting at Morning* are masterpieces of simplicity. The incisive nature-writing in the first poem perfectly sets the stage for the drama hinted at only in the last line, and the second poem brilliantly avoids the direct statement: again nature-description is used to heighten the sense of tension and emotion, and there is a world of meaning in the last line.

Browning's greatest poem of marital tragedy is undoubtedly *Andrea del Sarto*. This poem has been very variously interpreted, and the character of the "faultless painter" viewed from many different angles, but it seems clear that in his courageous, uncomplaining acceptance of an impossible situation we are again shown the heights to which human nature can attain.

He would not if he could blame his lovely wife Lucrezia; indeed, he cannot, he knows life too well to lay blame on any single individual:

> . . . In tragic life, God wot,
> No villain need be! passions spin the plot.[1]

The issue, he knows, is not in their hands:

> . . . We are in God's hand.
> How strange now, looks the life he makes us lead,
> So free we seem, so fettered fast we are!
> I feel he laid the fetter: let it lie.

Although he suffers all the pain of the artist longing for understanding and sympathy from the one who should be the first to give it, and finding it there never, he realizes how vain, in his case, such suffering is:

> .And yet how profitless to know, to sigh,
> "Had I been two, another and myself,
> Our head would have o'erlooked the world."
> . . . .
>
> Had you . . . given me soul
> We might have risen to Rafael, you and I.

But she has no soul to give, no artist's soul. She is not to blame, the capacity is not there, and she is beautiful, and has, after all, given him much:

[1] George Meredith, *Modern Love.*

> Nay, love, you did give all I asked, I think—
> More than I merit, yes, by many times.
> But had you—oh, with the same perfect brow,
> And perfect eyes, and more than perfect mouth,
> And the low voice my soul hears, as a bird
> The fowler's pipe, and follows to the snare—
> Had you, with these the same, but brought a mind!
> Some women do so. . . .

He has made the irretrievable mistake of so many artists, the mistake that can only lead to tragedy. Her perfect brow, perfect mouth, low voice, all her snaring beauty, blinded him to the truth he was to discover too late: she had no mind to bring with these physical attractions. And mind, soul, is the artist's supreme need. Without sympathetic mental companionship he is near shipwreck. And an enforced companionship that lacks this one essential is an hourly crucifixion. There are remedies for most human mistakes, but what is the remedy for the unhappy marriage? If marriages were as difficult to contract as to sever, there would be less disaster. In this monologue of poignant inner disaster the artist confesses all his weaknesses, all his faith. He knows his art should be enough:

> . . . Why do I need you?
> What wife had Rafael, or has Agnolo?

Nevertheless he owns:

I often am much wearier than you think,
This evening more than usual, and it seems
As if—forgive now—should you let me sit
Here by the window with your hand in mine
And look a half-hour forth on Fiesole,
Both of one mind, as married people use,
Quietly, quietly the evening through,
I might get up to-morrow to my work
Cheerful and fresh as ever.

Although he has long since faced his tragedy, it seems he has not yet fully accepted it, and still the ghosts of hope and the demons of regret torment him. A profound sadness is on his spirit:

. . . days decrease,
And autumn grows, autumn in everything.
Eh? The whole seems to fall into a shape
As if I saw alike my work and self
And all that I was born to be and do
A twilight-piece.

At last he is compelled to come face to face with his situation. At last he is in the throes of realization, after years of merely knowing. He has loved, and he has been mistaken. He must go forever alone. Yet he believes God is just, God cannot be mistaken. In some way he cannot see, there must be purpose and plan in his disaster. Now he must accept the broken dreams and rebuild from the ruins. Regret will not help him. So at last, after a sorrowful plea:

Come from the window, love—come in, at last,
Inside the melancholy little house
We built to be so gay with,

he reflects:

I am grown peaceful as old age to-night.
I regret nothing, I would change still less.
Since there my past lies, why alter it?

The poem celebrates a quiet, unseen courage.

Another poem of marital tragedy, *James Lee's Wife*, though a penetrating psychological study, pales beside *Andrea del Sarto.* Neither the form nor the diction has the dignity of the Italian painter's monologue, in spite of the wife's brave attempt to hold to her ideal of love, in spite of her courage in facing and striving to accept the pitiful situation. She tries by every means known to her to understand the origin of the tragedy, admits she must have been mistaken:

Well, and if none of these good things came,
What did the failure prove?
The man was my whole world, all the same,
With his flowers to praise, or his weeds to blame,
And either, or both, to love. . . .

The root of the tragedy, which she naturally cannot see, lies in the phrase, "the man was my whole world." But there are few who can understand this truth, only those who Mr. Aldous Huxley in his book *Ends and*

Means defines as the "non-attached." He wisely emphasizes the fact that:

> . . . sexual activities sometimes make for a realisation of the individual's unity with another individual, and, through that individual, with the reality of the world; sometimes, on the contrary, for an intensification of individual separateness. In other words, sex leads sometimes to non-attachment, and sometimes to attachment.

Earlier in the chapter he explains that:

> separateness is attachment, and without non-attachment no individual can achieve unity either with God, or, through God, with other individuals.

In other words, only in the "perfect freedom" of the Christian life can human relationships be perfect. There is a form of love, a deep and intense "human" love, that is free of the sin of possessiveness. The lovers, through their love for each other, love the world, see with an ever-increasing vision deep into and beyond the appearance of life, and are concerned with the enrichment of personality. Such love is not an end in itself, but a means to an end, and that end not selfish, as possessive love is, but altruistic. In this love, the problem of "non-attachment," torment of the saint and the artist, does not arise, because in it there is an element which is creative and real. The world is seen not in, but through, the object of love, is not narrowed, but infinitely expanded. As with spiritual experience, the test of a love is in its fruits; possessive love shuts out, while true love embraces, the wide world and all its glory and meaning.

Like Andrea del Sarto, James Lee's wife knows that for her autumn has come:

> My heart shrivels up and my spirit shrinks curled.
> But why must cold spread? but wherefore bring change
> To the spirit,
> God meant should mate his with an infinite range
> And inherit
> His power to put life in the darkness and cold?

Bravely she tries to spur herself on to courage:

> . . . Rejoice that man is hurled
> From change to change unceasingly,
> His soul's wings never furled!

But all her efforts at courage, understanding, philosophy, are vain; they cannot repair their broken marriage; what hope indeed can there be when she is compelled to reflect:

> There is nothing to remember in me,
> Nothing I ever said with a grace,
> Nothing I did that you care to see,
> Nothing I was that deserves a place
> In your mind. . . .

She has no choice but to set him free. In this case, as in every unhappy marriage, the mistake had been at the outset: they had been deluded by a mutual simple passion, knowing no need to look deeper, having indeed no vision to look beyond their own immediate desires. The disaster begins when, with the passing of years, it grows evident that passion alone cannot support a union; the incalculable element that distinguishes man from the animals has been ignored, and there can only be suffering. No marriage can survive unless it is a "marriage of true minds." The outer shell may be preserved, but within there is only hollow frustration, and the dusty seeds of untold tragedies. Both these poems are concerned with the vital moment, often evaded and its full implications ignored, over a long period of years, when the truth must at last be faced fully, and fully accepted. The human mind is provided with an almost limitless number of defences against unwelcome truth; day by day it unconsciously erects barriers. But a time comes at last when an unexpected crisis smashes down all that the mind has been so long building. It is a tragic moment. No wonder that subtle and most delicate instrument has busied itself so long with defences. What will remain when the fortifications of illusion are gone? This is the one failure every man and woman is fearful of; it seems to involve the failure of a whole life, "love that was life, life that was love."

Browning, because he was a great artist, offered no solution to these painful problems. His was only the task to portray life and human nature, searching for the truth. If art teaches or elucidates, it can only be by indirect methods. This is a universal law, involving more than art: a profound spiritual law too often broken, and always with disastrous results. Direct didactic methods must inevitably fail. For this reason, partly, Jesus taught in parables. There was no compulsion in his teaching, no insistence on soul-salvation. "He that hath an ear, let him hear." In the realm of the spirit, to which art is so near, men can be drawn, but never driven; this is where the artist-reformer so often fails. Afire with his own perception of truth, he is apt to forget that this truth was "given," not thrust upon him by some other fiery reformer; it was wrought of his own experience, or directly revealed, but there was no compulsion, in the usual sense of the word. It is indeed doubtful whether spiritual truths can ever be "taught": the seed is sown broadcast, the sower cannot tell whether it will fall on good ground or barren; he must be content with the knowledge that he has sown it. The main function of the poet is not to teach but to reveal life; art transcends morality. Although Browning as a Christian poet was fully aware of the only way out of the wilderness in which his multitudinous characters wandered, in his purely human dramas he was too good an artist to point the way. Although his convictions are implicit in all his writings, he declared his beliefs directly in his avowedly religious and philosophical works only. Here the field was clear. Yet even then he never wrote with intent to reform: he wrote because he could not do otherwise. An artist of his calibre has no choice. Throughout history certain individuals have been used for certain purposes; once conscious of this, their own personal lives are important to them only in so far as they observe in their development the progress of the purpose.

Browning was the poet of truth: it naturally follows that he was the great poet of love, and he, as no other poet, has proved the theory which Vladimir Solovyev in his book *Plato* suggests that Plato launched on the world but was unable to put into practical effect. Plato, Solovyev says, "who in theory towered over the majority of mortals, proved in real life to be an ordinary man."[1] He could not incarnate his transcendent ideal of love. It remained then for a Christian poet, living more than two thousand years later, to do this.

> Man can become divine only by the active power of an eternally existing Divinity and not of one coming into being, and that the way of the higher love, perfectly uniting male and female, the spiritual and the physical, is necessarily by its very principle a union or interaction of the divine and the human, or a divinely human process.

Browning's pursuit of truth was the search for God;

[1] Vladimir Solovyev, *Plato.*

he was always powerfully aware of the "eternally existing Divinity"; also he affirmed from the first an invincible belief in the divinity of love: Eros was for him always the "bridge-builder":

> Set free my love, and see what love can do
> Shown in my life—what work will spring from that! [1]

The development in his own life in the middle years—in all thinkers the years of crisis, when the whole meaning and purpose of life is put to the test—proved that Plato's ideal was attainable: the perfect union of man and woman was no vague philosopher's dream. Solovyev's "fifth way," "the perfect and final way of love which truly regenerates and deifies," Browning found. Remembering his experience, there is no need to fear that the attempt to incarnate the ideal must end in disaster. Browning's faith was such that he lived for fifteen magnificent years side by side with his ideal.

On the eve of their marriage, Elizabeth Barrett wrote to him:

> By to-morrow at this time, I shall have *you* only to love me—my beloved! You *only*. As if one said *God only*. And we shall have Him beside, I pray of Him.[2]

This is the Christian conception of love, and this the

[1] *In a Balcony*.
[2] *The Browning Love-Letters*.

reason why they could not fear any danger in living day by day with an ideal too many poets have held to be a dream not realizable on earth. But here God and the ideal are one: the ideal can fail only if God fails, and that is impossible.

CHAPTER III

THE POET OF ART AND OF NATURE

Yet nature is made better by no mean,
But nature makes that mean: so, over that art
Which you say adds to nature, is an art
That nature makes. . . .
. . . this is an art
Which does mend nature, change it rather, but
The art itself is nature.—*A Winter's Tale.*

AS in Browning's conception of love there is no final dualism between soul and body, so his conceptions of art, nature, life, were not three but one. There was no separate problem: all were aspects of a final unity. This is where the Christian poet inevitably prevails: his faith ever creates unity from apparent dualisms. God is the true and only centre; God is immanent in, while transcending, all aspects of life, therefore there must be final harmony. The discords are due only to imperfect hearing.

Life embraces art and nature; life is nature, nature life; art, being an interpretation of life, a reflection of nature, appears to be less than both, yet cannot be, since it enriches man's apprehension of life and heightens his appreciation of nature. The definitions can continue indefinitely; critics rend art and each other in their attempts at final clarifications: are we to accept "art for art's sake," or art for humanity's sake? Is art allied to Beauty, or shall we ignore Beauty, pursuing Truth only? Or are they, as Keats said, one and the same? Then what of Goodness? And if art is a-moral, what of them all? Is the function of art solely to reflect, not even interpret, life? All these, and a hundred and one similar problems, perplex artists, critics and the art-public, but Browning never seemed perplexed; he was content not to argue, he indulged in no intellectual broils; for him, art and his prosecution of it was life; he had no time to waste in profitless debate. He wrote poetry; he did not argue about it.

Nevertheless, his passion for art in every aspect, especially for painting and music, made him the greatest English poet of art. No other poet has devoted years of his life to writing of, learning of, and even working at, arts other than his own. Never has there been another poet with so wide a practical knowledge of painting, except, of course, Rossetti, who, however, was first a painter and second a poet, and possibly Blake, but Blake's art-knowledge is never revealed in his writings, as Browning's is. Poem after poem Browning devotes to painting and painters; so obsessed was he with the plastic arts that for some years after he and Elizabeth Barrett Browning arrived in Italy he worked strenuously at modelling, and studied the Italian painters so absorbedly that he found no time for writing, greatly to her distress. His writing about art, therefore, is not the writing of the amateur or the chilly professional critic: he plunges deep into the subject and writes from the inside; his poems about painting are the poems a painter turned poet would write, his poems about music the utterance of a musician suddenly given the gift of words.

> . . . such men
> Carry the fire, all things grow warm to them.[1]

Browning was possessed by the desire he voiced in *One Word More:*

> . . . of all the artists living, loving
> None but would forego his proper dowry,—
> Does he paint? he fain would write a poem,—
> Does he write? he fain would paint a picture,
> Put to proof art alien to the artist's.

This passion was allied to the desire to experience all, be all things, first voiced in *Pauline*. To such natures, the thought that there are heights unscalable, arts unattainable, and arts wherein a more vivid conception of life may perhaps be revealed, is intolerable. Again, and always, the search for truth is involved: only through exploration of every conceivable channel can the searcher in any degree satisfy himself; the one step of the way still unexplored may always be precisely the one where the key to the whole riddle is hidden. This passion, and the love for "life, the mere living,"

[1] *Bishop Blougram's Apology*.

the breathing of life's air in great draughts, never in gentle inhalations, accounts for Browning's intense preoccupation with other arts. And there is more than a hint of regret in stanza XII of the same poem:

> I shall never, in the years remaining,
> Paint you pictures, no, nor carve you statues,
> Make you music that should all-express me;
> So it seems: I stand on my attainment.
> This of verse alone, one life allows me;
> Verse and nothing else have I to give you,
> Other heights in other lives, God willing.

Naturally he could not appreciate the irony of a poet of his stature complaining that he had achieved "verse and nothing else."

It is inevitable, in spite of his preoccupation with other arts, that his greatest poems about art should be concerned with poets: the speaker in *Pauline* is a poet—we will not press the question as to whether the poem is or is not autobiographical. Had the poet wished it to be known, he would have made it clear. And in any case, such enquiry, and any subsequent conclusions, neither add to nor detract from the value of a work of art, which is complete in itself, a perfect new creation. A poet plays a large part in *Paracelsus*, the hero of *Sordello* is a poet, there is also the fine poem *Cleon*. But there are brilliant poems about painters. *Fra Lippo Lippi*, *Francis Furini*, *Andrea del Sarto*, *Pictor Ignotus*, and in many poems besides

Abt Vogler, *A Toccata at Galuppi's* and *Charles Avison* he writes with profound understanding of music from the musician's point of view. Then there are *Old Pictures in Florence*, *The Guardian Angel*, *Eurydice to Orpheus*, *A Likeness*, all concerned with painting.

In *Andrea del Sarto* the profound discontent of the artist with his achievement runs parallel with, aggravates, the human pain of the frustrated lover. He, the " faultless painter," is only too well aware of his shortcomings:

> . . . All is silver-grey
> Placid and perfect with my art: the worse!
> I know both what I want and what might gain.

He knows well that other painters, less technically perfect than he, have "the soul right"; they have achieved exactly what he lacks. It occurs to him, not unnaturally, since he is now fully facing his situation, that the love-frustration in his life may be partly responsible for the failure; too much energy is absorbed, no doubt, in profitless conflict, idle regret. Not only because he himself but because his art, too, suffers, he cries: "Why do I need you?" Greater men, Rafael, Agnolo, have not been so weak as to need a woman's love to help them to perfect their art. "And thus we half-men struggle." He has little but contempt for himself: he knows his art should be enough, and the very fact of the knowledge that it is not adds another weight to his already over-heavy burden. He passionately needs love, too:

> Let my hands frame your face in your hair's gold,
> You beautiful Lucrezia that are mine.

There his weakness lies, and too well he knows it. Better far if their love had ended long ago, in perfection. Always the same plaint, the same problem: love has been too weak to stand the test of time:

> You called me, and I came home to your heart.
> The triumph was, to have ended there. . . .

But somewhere there had always been a flaw, which he had been too blind to see. Now, seeing it at last, surely he should have strength enough to face and accept it: put love and his need of her aside, live only for his art, become the great painter he, with his technical gifts, could surely be. This is the obvious solution for the great man; Andrea del Sarto is not great enough. He can come to no terms with his problem: to abandon all thought of love and dedicate the remainder of his life to art is more than he is capable of doing. For him, the failure of love means the failure of life. Beside his need for perfect love, art fades into insignificance—another cause for suffering, for he is artist enough to be tormented by the betrayal. He, whom the world considers fortunate, for he is a very successful artist, is in fact a man divided against himself, and fatally weakened by the conflict. In this poem, contrary to his usual custom, Browning has not raised the problem, always uppermost in his mind, of the greatest good, the true duty. If he had, he might have questioned whether Andrea's "duty," entirely opposed to duty as accepted by the world, would be to leave his wife, not because she was unfaithful, the usual valid reason on which grounds for divorce or separation are based—implying that the physical aspect of marriage is the only one worthy of serious attention—but because—far graver in Browning's eyes—she was utterly inadequate, and not only did not further, but definitely, by the powerful hidden influences inherent in the close intimacy of marriage, retarded his art and his possibilities of achievement. In other words, she was slowly but surely undermining his soul. The relationship was, in the last resort, a degradation. Yet perhaps Andrea's attitude, condemned by some critics as weakness, was actually evidence of the greatest strength. He may have been mistaken, his solution to the problem may not have been the right one, yet there is a nobility of the highest order in the man who, while knowing his soul to be in peril, allows the danger to continue for what appears to him the essential good: the good of another human being, and the life of his own ideal. The innumerable factors involved in such a conflict cannot be hinted at even in a poem so profound as Browning's.

Love, passion, duty, art, the claims of the soul, the claims of the ideal, and throughout a steadfast background of religious faith:

> . . . At the end
> God, I conclude, compensates, punishes.

But this is the same doctrine of resignation and despair as in *Bifurcation:*

> Heaven repairs what wrongs earth's journey did.

No faith in life itself; no hope, no thought that life here might be heaven were we less blind. Andrea del Sarto had at some point in his life missed the vital opportunity; with deeper wisdom he would have discovered how to adjust his life, accepting the failure, and building a strong edifice from the ruins.

In *Pictor Ignotus* Browning writes of a disaster only an artist could understand, this time unquestionably a disaster of weakness. The painter of "endless cloisters and eternal aisles" has chosen to execute church decorations, to remain an unknown painter, rather than expose the work of his soul, the pictures he could have painted, to the criticism and painful misunderstanding of the world. Every creative artist will understand this shrinking; this it was that caused William Sharp, the literary critic, to publish all his intimate imaginative work under the pseudonym

Fiona Macleod. Nevertheless, in Browning's "unknown painter" there is a grave weakness: he really loves himself more than his art, and for fear of hurt to himself will not attempt the great good he might have achieved:

> At least no merchant traffics in my heart.

His heart is more important to him than the work he might have done, and he consoles himself with the thought that he has saved his tender feelings from injury, yet still the conviction that he "could have painted pictures like that youth ye praise so" irks him. But he has only himself to blame, could he but see: if his ideal of art had been strong enough he would have cared little for criticism.

Fra Lippo Lippi, crammed with vivid imagery, profound human understanding, flashes of beauty, fragments of philosophy, is a masterly poem, and a subject after Browning's own heart. The truant monk, the little starved boy saved at the age of eight from a world that in spite of his cloistered existence was never to leave him alone, was one of the worst of sinners, no doubt, but he became one of the greatest of painters. This was exactly the contradictory type of story to appeal to Browning. Who is to judge Filippo Lippi, a sinner in life, a saint in his art? Despite his lack of a moral sense, he had a true religion of his own, and a fine philosophy of art:

art was given by God to increase and enrich our perception of life:

> God uses us to help each other so,
> Lending our minds out. . . .

He has the gift of drawing human beings so that each face, each body, is revealed in a new light. His intensity urges him to express what he so passionately believes:

> . . . This world's no blot for us,
> Nor blank; it means intensely, and means good:
> To find its meaning is my meat and drink.

He cannot paint "beauty" only, nor yet soul only, as the Prior urges; he must paint truth. The Church protests; he should "paint the soul, never mind the legs and arms." But that, of course, is finally impossible, as Lippo, the great artist, knows well, and does not hesitate to say. Not for any church, any doctrine, will he perjure his soul, surrender his artistic integrity. He should never have been a monk, should never have submitted to any dogmatic religion: he is preeminently the independent artist of original mind, whose intuitions are direct messages from God; he needs no intermediary. So he is naturally at variance with the Church. Like all great artists, he is living before his time, a pioneer, and thus inevitably misunderstood and abused. He will not agree to the criticism of the Creator implied in the demand for purely "spiritual" art:

—The beauty and the wonder and the power,
The shapes of things, their colours, lights and shades,
Changes, surprises—and God made it all!
—For what? Do you feel thankful, ay or no,
For this fair town's face, yonder river's line,
The mountain round it and the sky above,
Much more the figures of man, woman, child
These are the frame to?

Either he must paint all he sees, or nothing. The Prior may protest as much as he will that his pictures do not "instigate to prayer." This, says Lippo, is not the function of art. Something far less than art would do to remind the people of matins, fasts, feast-days. There is no such obvious connection between art and religion. Again, if art is to teach, it must be indirectly only. Through his pictures, painted as he insists he must paint them, many may be led to see life, humanity, differently, and this, no doubt, though Lippi does not say so, may lead many to prayer. Life fully faced and considered becomes so momentous, so majestic and so tragic, that without faith, without prayer, it is no longer supportable. Fra Lippo Lippi knows that the function of art is to awaken men to life; he will have nothing to do with the claims of those who demand beauty, or pleasure, only.[1] And this, in the fifteenth century, when all painters were religious painters controlled almost entirely by the Church, was a

[1] Cf. Tolstoy, *What is Art?*

highly revolutionary and dangerous doctrine. Fra Lippo Lippi was no moralist, but his work had the true prophetic quality which is the test of greatness. Like all great men, he was a law to himself, towering above the commonplace judgments of the world.

Old Pictures in Florence, though marred here and there by Browning's one æsthetic failing, his peculiar, fantastic and often exasperating rhyming-devices, is a magnificent poem of art and its function, art and the public, reflections on immortality, and the temporal life. It begins with a perfect picture of Florence on a warm March day:

> River and bridge and street and square
> Lay mine, as much at my beck and call,
> Through the live translucent bath of air,
> As the sights in a magic crystal ball.

Contemplating the labour of soul and hand that had made the churches and galleries of Florence famous, the poet grieves for the wrongs the world inflicts, and has ever inflicted, on the artist:

> For oh! this world and the wrong it does!
> They are safe in heaven with their backs to it,
> The Michaels and Rafaels, you hum and buzz
> Round the works of, you of the little wit!
> Do their eyes contract to the earth's old scope,
> Now that they see God face to face,
> And have all attained to be poets, I hope?
>
> . . . .

Much they reck of your praise and you!
But the wronged great souls,—can they be quit
Of a world where their work is all to do,
Where you style them, you of the little wit,
Old Master This and Early the Other. . . .

So much for the world's judgment. Here they come, the blind art-critics, the sightless sight-seers, with their guide-books and their note-books, lumbering in where angels would hesitate to waft a wing lest they brush some rainbow-dust from the rare butterfly.

May I take upon me to instruct you?

. . . .

The Truth of Man, as by God first spoken,
Which the actual generations garble,
Was re-uttered, and Soul (which Limbs betoken)
And Limbs (Soul informs) made new in marble.

This, then, and no less, is the artist's task. It is the truth as first uttered by God, and now conveyed through paint and marble, that the blind lumberers are confronted with. Some, of course, may be enriched by what they see:

So, testing your weakness by their strength,
Your meagre charms by their rounded beauty,
Measured by Art in your breadth and length,
You learned—to submit is a mortal's duty.
When I say "you" 'tis the common soul,
The collective, I mean: the race of Man
That receives life in parts to live in a whole,
And grow here according to God's clear plan.

Growth came when, looking your last upon them all,
You turned your eyes inwardly one fine day. . . .

This is *one* function of art: to bring man to an understanding of himself through the portrayal of the invisible:

To bring the invisible full into play!
Let the visible go to the dogs—what matters?

"Faith is the substance of things hoped for, the evidence of things not seen." This does not necessarily conflict with Fra Lippo Lippi's insistence on painting the visible:

. . . nor soul helps flesh more, now than flesh helps soul.[1]

Browning rarely launches a direct attack on any section of society; this was not usually his method, but for once the common attitude to art had driven him to violence: he knew the divinity of art, the mission of the artist, and such a blundering attitude, indifferent, if not contemptuous or openly abusive, is in the nature of a blasphemy. In stanzas XXI and XXII he considers the doctrine of reincarnation, and refutes the theory held by many that he fully accepted the idea:

There's a fancy some lean to and others hate—
That, when this life is ended, begins
New work for the soul in another state,

[1] *Rabbi Ben Ezra.*

Where it strives and gets weary, loses and wins

. . . .

Through life after life in unlimited series. . . .

. . . .

Yet I hardly know. When a soul has seen
By the means of Evil that Good is best,
And, through earth and its noise, what is heaven's serene,
When our faith in the same has stood the test—
Why, the child grown man, you burn the rod,
The uses of labour are surely done;
There remaineth a rest for the people of God:
And I have had troubles enough, for one.

These stanzas are not quoted by theosophists writing to prove Browning one of their followers. Actually, he was a follower of God only; he submitted to no man-evolved sect.

The Guardian Angel is in many ways one of Browning's loveliest poems. There is a quality of divine weariness, the exhaustion of mind and soul known fully only to the artist and the saint; throughout, the poem breathes peace and suffering, but no purely human suffering, although the body inevitably suffers through so much stress of soul. If only the great angel guarding the child in the picture would leave him for a while and bend over the tired poet:

—And suddenly my head is covered o'er
With those wings, . . .
. . . and I shall feel thee guarding

Me, out of all the world; for me, discarding
Yon heaven thy home, that waits and opes its door.

. . . .

If this was ever granted, I would rest
My head beneath thine, while thy healing hands
Close covered both my eyes beside thy breast,
Pressing the brain which too much thought expands,
Back to its proper size again, and smoothing
Distortion down till every nerve had soothing,
And all lay quiet, happy and suppressed.

How soon all worldly wrong would be repaired!
I think how I should view the earth and skies
After thy healing, with such different eyes.

Strange words, it may seem, from the robust poet of optimism, the poet who, it is affirmed, believed that all was right with the world—just because his creation Pippa on her yearly holiday sang that it was! As well dismiss Browning as an optimist because of Pippa's words as Shakespeare as a pessimist because Hamlet condemned the world as a pestilential congregation of vapours. It is necessary to look deeper. Their philosophy was not so simple. Browning was a poet of all life; if he appears in the main an optimist, it is because of his Christianity. But because he was a poet, he was often a profoundly sad, profoundly disturbed and weary man. The poet, although greatly blessed, is never "lucky." He carries the sins of the world, a cross he can never lay down; a prototype of Man, he is Prometheus bound, enduring age-long torments for the liberation of humanity. His external conditions are nothing to him; the tragic yet divine inner drama for which he is cast absorbs him altogether. Every poet could echo Andrea del Sarto's words: "I often am much wearier than you think." His is not personal but world-sorrow, for which there is no solace. The "brain which too much thought expands" is never quiet. When Browning in youth longed to "live all life," he scarcely realized then that the fulfilment of that wish is inevitably the poet's fate: he lives a thousand lives beside his own. This is what Keats means when he speaks of the poet having no identity. There is no rest in such a state. So Browning, the man to whom life had brought so much good fortune, whom circumstances and environment had never thwarted, who had enjoyed a happy home-life, parents who understood him and desired his true good, whose marriage became the example of all a perfect marriage can be, was yet a tired, distracted man, in this poem echoing Shelley's plaint that he could "lie down like a tired child and weep away his life of care":

> Let me sit all the day here, that when eve
> Shall find performed thy special ministry,
> And time come, for departure, thou, suspending,
> Thy flight, mayst see another child for tending,
> Another still, to quiet and retrieve.

Strange paradox: the poet alone of men attains to full maturity, yet he alone knows throughout his life the loneliness and weariness of the child, his wisdom no infallible solace for his desolation.

The short poem *Eurydice to Orpheus* may be quoted in full: it is a perfect miniature of condensed power and beauty:

> But give them me, the mouth, the eyes, the brow,
> Let them once more absorb me! One look now
> Will lap me round for ever, not to pass
> Out of its light, though darkness lie beyond.
> Hold me but safe again within the bond
> Of one immortal look! All woe that was
> Forgotten, and all terror that may be
> Defied—no past is mine, no future: look at me!

In *Francis Furini* (*Parleyings with Certain People of Importance in their Day*) Browning returns to a favourite theme: his reverence for the human body, and, as an inevitable corollary, his hatred of cant and false morality. Furini, a famous painter noted especially for his nudes, turns priest at the age of forty, and thence deeply regrets his past work. But how, argues Browning, could he r ghtly feel shame for:

> . . . pictures rife
> With record, in each rendered loveliness,
> That one appreciative creature's debt
> Of thanks to the Creator more or less,
> Was paid according as heart's will had met

> Hand's power in Art's endeavour to express
> Heaven's most consummate of achievements, bless
> Earth by a semblance of the seal God set
> On woman his supremest work. . . .

Surely at his death his vision must have been purged, and he cured of his misunderstanding, seeing his gift in its true light. Thence Browning, who is sometimes thought of as a romantic poet only, a weighty philosophical thinker, or a religious writer, but scarcely ever as a modern, launches into a virulent attack on hypocritical morality, using words to match the foulness of his subject, in typically modern style:

> A satyr masked as matron—makes pretence
> To the coarse blue-fly's instinct—can perceive
> No better reason why she should exist—
> God's lily-limbed and blush-rose-bosomed Eve—
> Than as a hot-bed for the sensualist
> To fly-blow with his fancies, make pure stuff
> Breed him back filth—this were not crime enough?

In stanza VII he suggests to Furini how he should have prayed, understanding the body as the temple of the spirit:

> ". . . Bounteous God
> Deviser and Dispenser of all gifts
> To soul and sense,—in Art the soul uplifts
> Man's best of thanks! What but Thy measuring-rod
> Meted forth heaven and earth? more intimate,
> Thy very hands were busied with the task
> Of making, in this human shape, a mask—

A match for that divine. Shall love abate
Man's wonder? Nowise! True—true—all too true—
No gift but, in the very plenitude
Of its perfection, goes maimed, misconstrued
By wickedness or weakness: still, some few
Have grace to see Thy purpose, strength to mar
Thy work by no admixture of their own,
—Limn truth, not falsehood, bid us love alone
The type untampered with, the naked star!"

Browning knows well that true art "rouses no desires it does not in the same moment satisfy,"[1] if it does otherwise, the sin is in the observer. Purity, no less than lust, can be a passion, and it is this passion, this intense reverence for the body, its beauty and significance, that rouses Browning to fury. The foulest words in this cause are purged and justified by the end for which they are used: the regenerating fire has burned them clean; it is a case where an absolute evil becomes a positive good: here good can only be done by portraying evil in all its foulness; to evade or attempt to modify the reality and extent of the evil would be to condone it. Browning was not a man for half-measures or compromise; his passionate love of good was at least equalled by his intense hatred of evil, and false morality, abuse of a high value, roused his most fervent hatred. He would have nothing to do with vice masquerading as virtue, and prudery

[1] G. Wilson Knight, *The Christian Renaissance.*

shocked him: he was too sound a psychologist not to understand its true meaning. Again, in this poem, the confusion of values horrifies him: the criticism of the Creator implied in the view that this miraculous soul-case, the body, can in itself be evil. . . . The rest of the poem develops into a profound philosophical rumination on good and evil.

There is little justification in the belief that Browning's later poems are duller, dryer, less poetical than the earlier ones. They are more profound, but that is as it should be, yet none so obscure as his third work, *Sordello.* If they have lost a little in lyrical beauty, which is questionable, they have gained in strength; what they may have lost in youthful élan they have certainly gained in maturity. He remains to the end the vital poet of life. His later work is less popular because less well-known, less accessible; most of the usual editions end with *The Ring and the Book*, and the poems from 1870 onwards are available only in more expensive volumes. It is interesting in passing to wonder what kind of a poem Wordsworth would have produced on the subject that inspired *Francis Furini.* Considered nowadays a more noteworthy poet than Browning, yet surely it must be conceded that many urgent problems, meat and drink to a poet of Browning's robust calibre, would have caused Wordsworth considerable nausea and moral pain. There is a tendency in Wordsworth to do what Jude in Hardy's novel *Jude the Obscure* did on his first visit to Oxford: resolutely turn away from any aspect that conflicted with his ideal. But Browning was "ever a fighter." In *Prospice* he cried:

I would hate that death bandaged my eyes, and forebore,
And made me creep past.
No! let me taste the whole of it, fare like my peers
The heroes of old,
Bear the brunt. . . .

He would never bandage his eyes, he would taste the whole, bear the brunt, of whatever life might demand of him. His attitude to the unpleasant is largely in line with modern thought, which inclines even to the belief that ugliness, sordidness and vice prevail over beauty and goodness. Though this was not Browning's view, he was fully conscious of the reality of ugliness and evil, and did not shrink from portraying it in its true colours.

Stopford Brooke in his study *The Poetry of Robert Browning* begins with a comparison between "the two great Victorian poets" Browning and Tennyson. Comparison is not by any means the best form of criticism, yet sometimes it is necessary for the purpose of pointing an argument. My own reason for drawing any comparison here between these poets is to stress the unique timelessness, universality and breadth of Browning's work, as opposed to the topical quality of much of Tennyson's and Wordsworth's. It is perfectly true, as Stopford Brooke says, that

> there is scarcely a trace in his (Browning's) work of any vital interest in the changes of thought and feeling in England during the sixty years[1] of his life, such as appear everywhere in Tennyson. No one would know from his poetry . . . that the science of life and its origins had been revolutionised in the midst of his career . . . that the whole aspect of theology had been altered, or that the democratic movement had taken so many new forms. . . . They scarcely existed for him—transient elements of the world, merely national, not universal.

This, in my view, alone proves Browning the greatest of these three poets. It was not that he ignored or belittled these aspects of life; it was simply that he lived on a mountain, and, thus far removed from and above the strange activities of men, was able to see them in exact perspective, able to judge precisely which values were worthy of poetry and which divorced from any eternal or universal significance. The great poet shares with the prophet this gift of assessing final values; he lives not only in the present, but, in some way not rationally explicable, in past, present and future simultaneously. Hence much of his unpopularity: he dismisses as unimportant many things for which the good citizen swears he would

[1] This must refer to his writing-life. Browning lived to be seventy-seven.

give his life. As for the changes in religious thought during Browning's lifetime, his faith was too deeply rooted for this to affect him. "Earth changes, but thy soul and God stand sure."[1] The Christian, firmly rooted and grounded in faith, is not shaken by theological or scientific argument. The rationalist battles leave him unmoved; he listens with polite interest to modernist debates, notes the latest theories on the miracles, remarks that a certain professor has advanced a brilliant new theory on the Virgin Birth, that another has written on the Empty Tomb. He is not troubled, the demon of intellectual doubt can never find a way in. Browning was this kind of Christian; new theories naturally interested him, he was too passionately the poet of humanity not to sympathize with every new development of human thought, but he had supremely the mystic's gift for sifting the grain from the chaff.

One view of art is expressed briefly in the words in *Pippa Passes:*

> . . . One may do whate'er one likes
> In Art: the only thing is, to make sure
> That one does like it—which takes pains to know.

This coincides exactly with Tolstoy's passionate and recurrent plea for sincerity in *What is Art?* Sincerity, he affirms, is the acid test. At the same time, this immediately involves the difficult question of taste:

[1] *Rabbi Ben Ezra.*

an artist may sincerely like and enjoy working at something which cannot be classed as true art. Tolstoy devotes his third chapter entirely to varying definitions of art, and ends by saying:

> However strange it may seem . . . in spite of the mountains of books written about art, no exact definition of art has been constructed. And the reason for this is that the conception of art has been based on the conception of beauty.

Browning's art was not based on this conception: his concern was with truth (God); beauty inevitably followed.

> When religious perception guides a people's art beauty inevitably results, as has always been the case when men have seized a fresh perception of life and its purpose.[1]

Cleon, again, deals with art and life. The poet Cleon writes of the heightened perceptions and consequent heightened capacity for joy in the artist, of the meaning of life, apprehended in its fullness only by him, yet grieves that this very fact of his increased awareness produces his sense of frustration: the artist can continue to portray life's joys, love's raptures, long after his physical powers allow him to experience them in actuality, and this imaginative knowledge, allied to actual incapacity, is torture. "Life's inadequate to

[1] Introduction to *What is Art?* by Aylmer Maude.

joy." The whole poem cries out for a full tasting of joy; the word occurs and recurs throughout, in varying contexts, and Cleon, scarcely less a philosopher than a poet, reflects on the whole meaning of this strange pattern wherein, to quote Andrea del Sarto:

> . . . a man's reach should exceed his grasp,
> Or what's a heaven for?

In essence, there is an echo from *Pauline:* "I cannot be immortal, nor taste all." The fundamental argument of the poem is a plea for the necessity of another life beyond death, because life proves so inadequate, so tormenting indeed, and offers the richest understanding of its possibilities to men when their physical powers are decaying. It cannot be regarded as anything but incomplete: "On the earth the broken arcs; in the heaven a perfect round."[1] Our chief pain, Cleon reflects, is due to incomplete vision, the incapacity to see the whole:

> For, what we call this life of men on earth,
> This sequence of the soul's achievements here,
> Being, as I find much reason to conceive,
> Intended to be viewed eventually
> As a great whole, not analysed to parts,
> But each part having a reference to all,—
> How shall a certain part, pronounced complete,
> Endure effacement by another part?

[1] *Abt Vogler.*

"Tout est dangereux ici-bas, et tout est necessaire."[1] The danger and the pain do not cancel out the necessity. The mystic, the poet, the philosopher, the saint, are all working in the cause of unity, working to prove the necessity for all the apparently conflicting pieces of the pattern. And, Cleon argues, life is growth: "Why stay we on the earth unless to grow?" But towards life's end we have grown too much; life on earth can no longer enclose that which has grown too big for it, and at last the soul is ready for the wider life. The fact that Cleon is not a Christian—he was a contemporary of St. Paul, but not a convert—cannot affect the vital Christian philosophy of the poem:

> . . . Man might live at first
> The animal life: but is there nothing more?
> In due time, let him critically learn
> How he lives; and, the more he gets to know
> Of his own life's adaptabilities,
> The more joy-giving will his life become.
> Thus man, who hath this quality, is best.

But Cleon is tormented by doubts which Christianity would have quieted. At the end he cries, why has not Zeus revealed the existence of a life beyond this death he dreads? "He must have done so, were it possible." If he had heard of the Resurrection, it had not convinced him, indeed, "their doctrine could be held by no sane man." Yet this Paulus of whom he speaks

[1] Voltaire, *Zadig*.

rather with indifference writes passionately of the reality of the life Cleon craves:

> For as in Adam all die, so also in Christ shall all be made alive. . . . For this corruptible must put on incorruption, and this mortal must put on immortality. But when this corruptible shall have put on immortality, then shall come to pass the saying that is written, Death is swallowed up in victory. O death, where is thy sting? O grave, where is thy victory? . . . Thanks be to God, which giveth us the victory through our Lord Jesus Christ.[1]

Of the poems on music, *Abt Vogler* towers high above the rest, with *Charles Avison* some way below. There is in *Abt Vogler* the sense that the poem has written itself: the method, structure, rhythm, rhyme, all fuse into an inevitable style matching the grandeur and dignity of the theme. The first lines at once set the pace: the whole poem moves with a measured tread in essence similar to the procession of the Meistersinger in Wagner's great opera:

> Would that the structure brave, the manifold music I
> build,
> Bidding the organ obey, calling the keys to their work,
> Claiming each slave of the sound, at a touch, as when
> Solomon willed
> Armies of angels that soar, legions of demons that lurk,
> Man, brute, reptile, fly,—alien of end and of aim,
> Adverse, each from the other heaven-high, hell-deep
> removed,—

[1] 1 *Corinthians* xv. 53, 54, 55, 57.

Should rush into sight at once as he named the ineffable
Name,
And pile him a palace straight, to pleasure the princess he
loved.

This is the pace proper to a master of so mighty a musical instrument as the organ, and here, in the first stanza, the whole breadth and scope of his theme is suggested, soaring from earth to heaven, plunging to hell, a poem of art, philosophy, religion, and, as ever with Browning, the soul. There is the marriage of earth and heaven, union preceding the birth of an art-form, outlined in the fourth stanza:

And the emulous heaven yearned down, made effort to
reach the earth
As the earth had done her best, in my passion, to scale
the sky. . . .

then, in his creation, "earth had attained to heaven, there was no more near nor far." And all has been achieved through him, his touch on the keys, and the power of music:

All through my keys that gave their sound to a wish of my
soul,
All through my soul that praised as its wish flowed visibly
forth,
All through music and me! . . .

He acknowledges the omnipresent, omnipotent Power behind his great gift:

But here is the finger of God, a flash of the will that can,
Existent behind all laws that made them, and lo! they
are. . . .

Yet this "palace of music"[1] will not endure in fact, since it has been extemporization only. "Never to be again!" The thought that others as good may flow from his fingers is but small comfort. Nevertheless, this beauty, this momentary flash of truth he has apprehended and created, cannot be lost:

There shall never be one lost good!
What was, shall live as before.

This echoes the thought in the closing lines of Francis Thompson's *Hound of Heaven:*

All which thy child's mistake
Fancies as lost, I have stored for thee at home;

in Hopkins's *Leaden Echo and Golden Echo:*

Yes, I can tell such a key, I do know such a place
Where whatever's prized and passes of us, everything
that's fresh and fast-flying of us, seems to us sweet of
us and swiftly away with, done away with, undone. . .

. . . .

[1] It is interesting to note here that Professor Wilson Knight, in his invaluable book *Principles of Shakespearian Production*, writes of a Shakespeare play and its true production as "a sort of spiritual edifice . . . a performance is therefore not simply a sequence but architectonic, and makes a mind-building. In *Abt Vogler* Browning imagines an organ as making of great music a mystic building; and in Coleridge's *Kubla Khan* the paradisal dome could be 'built in air' by 'symphony and song'."

Never fleets more, fastened with the tenderest truth
To its own best being and its loveliness of youth. . . .

. . . .

. . . the thing we freely forfeit is kept with fonder a care,
Fonder a care kept than we could have kept it, kept
Far with fonder a care (and we, we should have lost it) finer, fonder,
A care kept.—Where kept? Do but tell us where kept, where—
Yonder.—What high as that! We follow, now we follow
Yonder, yes yonder, yonder,
Yonder.

The Christian poet "can tell such a key," there is no fear of ultimate loss. The same thought occurs in *Charles Avison:*

. . . Never dream
That what once lived shall ever die!

and in *The Ring and the Book* Pompilia knows that not even death can destroy a work once given to God:

O lover of my life, O soldier-saint,
No work begun shall ever pause for death!
Love will be helpful to me more and more
I' the coming course, the new path I must tread.

Neither life nor death has power over eternal values: here there is neither loss nor separation:

Tell him that if I seem without him now,
That's the world's insight! Oh, he understands!
He is at Civita—do I once doubt
The world again is holding us apart?

"The world." The whole world "lies in the hand of the Evil One," but the power of love and faith vanquishes the devil and his crippling emphases on time and space.

> . . . no beauty, nor good, nor power
> Whose voice has gone forth, but each survives for the melodist
> When eternity affirms the conception of an hour.[1]

If God has heard it, it can never be lost. Abt Vogler consoles himself with the customary assurance of the Christian, and finally of the artist:

> And what is our failure here but a triumph's evidence
> For the fulness of the days? Have we withered or agonised?
> Why else was the pause prolonged but that singing might issue thence?
> Why rushed the discords in, but that harmony should be prized?
> Sorrow is hard to bear, and doubt is slow to clear,
> Each sufferer says his say, his scheme of the weal or woe:
> But God has a few of us whom he whispers in the ear;
> The rest may reason and welcome: 'tis we musicians know.

Again, there is no doubt of the artist's divine mission. As Tolstoy says:[2]

> Humanity unceasingly moves forward from a lower, more partial, and obscure understanding of life, to one more general and more lucid. And in this, as in every movement,

[1] *Abt Vogler.*
[2] *What is Art?*

there are leaders—those who have understood the meaning of life more clearly than others.

Unhappily, while the world is ready, eager, to accept the leaders of materialistic movements: great statesmen, soldiers, financiers, and so on, the spiritual leaders are invariably regarded with suspicion, treated with contempt, indifference, or deliberate cruelty, and every kind of pressure is brought to bear to prevent them fulfilling their purpose. In the last chapter of his interesting book *The Modern Mind* Mr. Michael Roberts points the differences between the outlook of Church and State, and between the varying qualities of spiritual and materialistic leaders:

> The men best qualified for the executive work of government are not those who are best qualified for moral and spiritual leadership. . . . Every Government tends to become conservative. It is concerned with immediate material needs, not with distant objectives; it relies upon force rather than persuasion, it is concerned with things that are material, and its language is the language of law and not of poetry. . . .
>
> The Church must always be, in some sense, the enemy of the State: if it shows a real power of leadership it must continually raise new problems for the executive. It tries to develop each person, it does not aggrandise the State. . . . It aims at a sharpening of the individual conscience, not at the speedy punishment of the wrongdoer. It must always oppose the methods of coercion that are characteristic of law.

In the same chapter he also stresses the creative nature of religion as opposed to the conservative, static, even retrogressive, nature of law and the State. This hide-bound condition of society was precisely what Jesus came to overthrow, what St. Paul laboured passionately to supersede, and this is the eternal conflict that Christianity produces. The law may be well enough, but only as a temporary measure. There is a more perfect way. Jesus said:

Think not that I am come to destroy the law, or the prophets; I am not come to destroy, but to fulfil.[1]

He knew that all the principles of true growth were there, already embodied in the law, but the law itself was not fully understood. The Kingdom of Heaven is potentially within everyone; chaos prevails through lack of understanding of the laws governing growth:

The action that is really good is not the outcome of the existing moral code, but is more likely to lead to a revision of that code. It is a new discovery, and it is likely to be opposed by the State. The object of the State is to conserve, the object of a Church is to create. The State is, at the best, a reflection of average conscientious intelligent opinion. The business of a Church is to foster the seed from which new life can grow.[2]

This explains the need for the man of genius to become

[1] *Gospel according to St. Matthew* v. 17.
[2] Michael Roberts, *The Modern Mind.*

a law to himself, the reason why he must fully realize and accept the responsibility this involves. The prophet, the pioneer, is by his very nature destined to outgrow the law; hence his apparent immorality. The true laws of growth must of necessity often transcend a morality only man-conceived, conceived by "average conscientious intelligent opinion," in short. Therefore "all things are lawful unto me," says St. Paul, "but all things are not expedient." The pioneer must always beware in what way he reveals *in action* the beliefs he holds so passionately, otherwise he may defeat the very cause he lives to serve. There is always a profound antinomy between the conception of the ideal and the practice of it, and the only solution to so tormenting a dualism lies in Christianity itself: "be ye perfect." . . . The Christian poet, prophet, reformer, is often condemned as unpractical. What is his solution to the immediate urgent problems confronting the modern world? His theories may be all very splendid, but is he not fiddling while Rome burns? Christian pacifism, for example. This remote ideal of universal love, the brotherhood of man, peace on earth—all very beautiful, no doubt—dreams of a Utopia always have been beautiful, but how is the remote ideal to be brought into practice? How is human nature to be changed—if it ever can be changed—quickly enough to save Europe from its immediate peril? The Christian answer has to be that the idealist cannot work but for the future, for the slow, but, he is convinced, certain, perfectibility of humanity. Spiritual progress is inevitably slow; even if there is a sudden leap into reality by means of conversion, the subsequent growth in the soul is slow and laborious. Conversion in itself does not perfect a soul, it only points the way to perfection. And if each individual aims at perfection, the answer to every problem will inevitably come, exactly according to the measure of his advancement. The mystics from time immemorial have asserted that their problems "solve themselves," that no decision is ever arrived at by hard thinking. The solutions come when thought is quiescent. Therefore, if the man of genius accepts the basic principles of Christianity, he must inevitably know when and to what extent he should overthrow the law, sacrificing the lesser for the truly greater good.

The poet's Utopia does seem a remote ideal, yet it is simply a return to the Golden Age, to the "time of man's innocency," with perhaps the added grandeur and dignity of the long experience of suffering since the Fall.

> Ce que nous voyons autour de nous n'est plus que l'ombré de la Nature originelle. Comme un enfant a qui l'on a donné une montre, l'homme a voulu démonter le merveilleux instrument et y a jeté la confusion. [1]

[1] Albert Béguin, *L'Âme Romantique et le Rêve.*

And it is the poet "qui a la presentiment de notre essence vraie."

There are profound reflections on art in *Fifine at the Fair*, and a wonderful passage on music:

. . . Words struggle with the weight
So feebly of the False, thick element between
Our soul, the True, the Truth! which, but that intervene
False show of things, were reached as easily by thought
Reducible to word, as now by yearnings wrought
Up with thy fine free force, oh Music, that canst thrid
Electrically win a passage through the lid
Of earthly sepulchre, our words may push against,
Hardly transpierce as thou. . . .

The same thought is expressed briefly in *Charles Avison:*

There is no truer truth obtainable
By Man than comes of music.

Here Browning is not content with writing of music only: he ends the poem with a musical quotation, to be played (how Browning's whole personality vibrates in the word!) "lustily." *Charles Avison*, as Sydney Grew in *The British Musician* and elsewhere has continually pointed out, is not appreciated as it should be. Doubtless it lies under the shadow of Browning's other work of round about this period, and, again, quite unjustly; it has beauty, profundity—which goes without saying—often the light lyrical touch still, and it begins with an exquisite fancy about the bird, the sure messenger of spring, who comes among the fast-falling snows of late winter to steal a fragment to help build his nest. Browning's love for birds, and especially for his pet owl, is well known; only a more than ordinary bird-lover could write so sympathetically, convey in a few lines so living a picture of a bird's labours. The main characteristics of Browning's work are all summarized in this poem: his keen knowledge of psychology, evidenced in the associative method of thought outlined in the first four stanzas, his preoccupation with character, his philosophy of life and art, his love for, and inner understanding of, music, his insight into all forms of life. There is a good definition of the function of music in stanza VII:

> . . . To match and mate
> Feeling with knowledge,—make as manifest
> Soul's work as Mind's work, turbulence as rest,
> Hates, loves, joys, woes, hopes, fears, that rise and sink
> Ceaselessly, passion's transient flit and wink,
> A ripple's tinting or a spume-sheet's spread
> Whitening the wave,—or to strike all this life dead.
> Run mercury into a mould like lead,
> And henceforth have the plain result to show—
> How we Feel, hard and fast as what we Know—
> This were the prize and is the puzzle!—which
> Music essays to solve. . . .

In Browning's later work especially, his thought and method are quite in accord with most of the principles of modernism in poetry: intellectualism, obscurity, economy of diction, realism, peculiarities of structure and imagery, often crudity and even ugliness, all these qualities are recurrent; moreover, there is no subject he would reject if he saw in it eternal significance. It is not the matter but the manner that reveals the true poet. His poetry is innocent of the moralizing that often mars Wordsworth; it is as if he lives the life he writes of while writing, instead of standing aside as a spectator and discoursing on it. Much has been said of Wordsworth as the great nature mystic, but Browning's mysticism has been rather generally overlooked, when, in fact, he was a mystic in the best sense of the word, seeing God not only in "every bush and tree afire," but in every human face, every situation, every form of life, and having pre-eminently the mystic's gift of identification:

> I can live all the life of plants. . . .
>
> . . . .
>
> I can mount with the bird
> Leaping airily the pyramid of leaves. . . .
>
> . . . .
>
> Or like a fish breathe-in the morning air
> In the misty sun-warm water; or with flowers
> And trees can smile in light at the sinking sun.[1]

And in his contacts with humanity, like Whitman—

[1] *Pauline.*

with whom there are throughout many affinities—he does not ask the sufferer how he feels, he becomes the sufferer. He lives a myriad lives.

Commensurate with Browning's passion for art is his passion for nature, and for obvious reasons:

> Car la Vie est une, la même partout: la vie des plantes et celle des espèces animales s'organisent selon la même rhythme qui préside aux grandes periodes de la Nature: années, jours, heures. La Vie n'est autre chose que cet accord avec les relations polaires et harmonieuses des grandes forces universelles.[1]

The great poet of life is inevitably a poet of nature. He sees in nature not scenery only, not grandeur only; he does not search for magnificent views or strange phenomena; the least as well as the greatest of nature's manifestations is miraculous to him, for nature is the visible garment of the invisible God, and although this is rarely, if ever, clearly stated in Browning's nature poetry—it would hardly be possible to "state it clearly"—the sense of divine significance permeates all his nature writing.

Pauline, *Paracelsus*, and *Sordello*—*Sordello* especially—contain some of his loveliest descriptive passages. The following lines from *Pauline* breathe the spirit of the day when winter's end is certain at last:

[1] Albert Béguin, *L'Âme Romantique et le Rêve.*

Thou wilt remember one warm morn when winter
Crept aged from the earth, and spring's first breath
Blew soft from the moist hills; the black-thorn boughs,
So dark in the bare wood, when glistening
In the sunshine were white with coming buds,
Like the bright side of a sorrow, and the banks
Had violets opening from sleep like eyes.

This is exquisite writing: the vivid imagery, the apt epithets, the profound feeling for the first stirring of spring caught in and transmitted by these few lines makes it unique even in poetry. The line, "blew soft from the moist hills," blows the precise sense of the early spring morning into the reader's mind. There is a similar feeling in the lines from *Paracelsus:*

As one spring wind unbinds the mountain-snow
And comforts violets in their hermitage.

In *Paracelsus*, too, is the glorious description of dawn:

See, morn at length. The heavy darkness seems
Diluted; grey and clear without the stars;
The shrubs bestir and rouse themselves, as if
Some snake, that weighed them down all night, let go
His hold; and from the East, fuller and fuller,
Day, like a mighty river, flowing in. . . .

I know of no more vivid picture of dawn, chill and clear and strange, although the lines from William Morris's poem *Summer Dawn*, are akin:

The heavy elms wait, and restless and cold
The uneasy wind rises. . . .

Then there is in *Paracelsus* the stirring song "Over the sea our galleys went," the lines rocking and rolling with the rhythm of the waves, and the delightful little picture of bird and animal life:

> Where the glossy kingfisher
> Flutters when noon-heats are near,
> Glad the shelving banks to shun,
> Red and steaming in the sun,
> Where the shrew-mouse with pale throat
> Burrows, and the speckled stoat;
> Where the quick sandpipers flit
> In and out the marl and grit
> That seems to breed them, brown as they:
> Nought disturbs its quiet way,
> Save some lazy stork that springs
> Trailing it with legs and wings,
> Whom the shy fox on the hill
> Rouses, creep he ne'er so still.

No wonder Paracelsus exclaims:

> They loose my heart, those simple words,
> Its darkness passes, which nought else could touch.

There is another passage reminiscent of the lines quoted from *Pauline:*

> Then all is still; earth is a wintry clod:
> But spring-wind, like a dancing psaltress, passes
> Over its breast to waken it, rare verdure
> Buds tenderly upon rough banks, between
> The withered tree-roots, and the cracks of frost,
> Like a smile striving with a wrinkled face.

For once, at the end of this lovely spring-description, there is a direct reference to the divine:

> . . . God renews
> His ancient rapture. Thus he dwells in all,
> From life's minute beginnings, up at last
> To man. . . .

Then Browning writes finely of man's attitude to, and relation with, nature:

> . . . Man, once descried, imprints for ever
> His presence on all lifeless things: the winds
> Are henceforth voices, wailing or a shout,
> A querulous matter or a quick gay laugh,
> Never a senseless gust now man is born.
> The herded pines commune and have deep thoughts
> A secret they assemble to discuss
> When the sun drops behind their trunks which glare
> Like grates of hell: the peerless cup afloat
> Of the lake-lily is an urn, some nymph
> Swims bearing high above her head: no bird
> Whistles unseen. . . .
>
> . . . .
>
> The morn has enterprise, deep quiet droops
> With evening, triumph takes the sunset hour,
> Voluptuous transport ripens with the corn. . . .

Man, in whom "God is glorified," has somewhat changed the face of nature, although, paradoxically, nature remains ever indifferent to man. Yet the advent of man ushers in a new era even in the world of nature. The poem ends with a magnificent nature metaphor:

. . . If I stoop
Into a dark tremendous sea of cloud,
It is but for a time; I press God's lamp
Close to my breast; its splendour, soon or late
Will pierce the gloom: I shall emerge one day.

But of these three early poems *Sordello* is richest in nature-writing; so many, so various, and often so lengthy are these lovely descriptive passages, that choice is difficult. The scene of the poem is vividly set, the poet writes with a painter's intense awareness of colour, form and grouping. The picture of the sunset almost at the beginning is typical:

. . . That autumn eve was stilled:
A last remains of sunset dimly burned
O'er the far forests, like a torch-flame turned
By the wind back upon its bearer's hand
In one long flare of crimson; as a brand
The woods beneath lay black.

Because *Sordello* is throughout a poem of intensity, of swift, powerful action (although the true inner drama is concerned with so profound and obscure a matter as the development of a soul, the outer setting is swift, forceful, colourful), all the imagery is necessarily of a similar nature. This is inevitable. The poet does not deliberately choose his metaphors to suit his subject; being permeated with the subject, the appropriate imagery insinuates itself. Here is a passage akin to *The Eve of St. Agnes*, one of Keats's richest descriptive poems, dyed throughout with the deep and vivid colours of a pre-Raphaelite tapestry:

> . . . a castle built amid
> A few low mountains; firs and larches hid
> Their main defiles, and rings of vine-yard bound
> The rest. Some captured creature in a pound
> Whose artless wonder quite precludes distress,
> Secure beside in its own loveliness,
> So peered with airy head, below, above,
> The castle at its toils, the lapwings love
> To glean among at grape-time. Pass within.
> A maze of corridors contrived for sin,
> Dusk winding-stairs, dim galleries got past,
> You gain the inmost chambers, gain at last
> A maple-panelled room: that haze which seems
> Floating about the panel, if there gleams
> A sunbeam over it, will turn to gold
> And in the light-graven characters unfold
> The Arab's wisdom everywhere; what shade
> Marred them a moment, those slim pillars made
> Cut like a company of palms to prop
> The roof, each kissing top entwined with top,
> Leaning together; in the carver's mind
> Some knot of bacchanals, flushed cheek combined
> With straining forehead, shoulders purpled, hair
> Diffused between, who in a goat-skin bear
> A vintage. . . .

This kind of descriptive writing, though the latter part is not, strictly speaking, descriptive of natural beauty, can be ranked among poetry of the highest order, because, to quote Browning himself, "nor soul helps flesh more, now, than flesh helps soul." This is body irradiated by soul, the least common object suffused with light. Many modern poets fail here: they lack the powerful life-sense, the sense of the more than life within life, and manifested in the common things of life, that unfailingly possessed Browning; that is why they confuse values and believe that realism consists in writing only of ordinary things, that the choice of such themes *in itself* constitutes "seeing life whole" and with unflinching honesty. Browning, while writing this passage in *Sordello*, lived intensely in the scene. Perhaps, after all, the final test of art is intensity, as Keats believed.

Again, in the following lines how vivid is the sensuous appeal:

> He climbed . . .(June at deep) some close ravine
> 'Mid clatter of its million pebbles sheen,
> Over which, singing soft, the runnel slipped
> Elate with rains. . . .

Consummate "unpremeditated art" in the last three words. Then the opening of the second Book, so perfect a picture, again, of winter's end:

> The woods were long austere with snow: at last
> Pink leaflets budded on the beech, and fast
> Larches, scattered through pine-tree solitudes,
> Brightened, as in the slumbrous heart of the woods

As if God's messenger thro' the close wood screen
Plunged and replunged his weapon at a venture,
Feeling for guilty thee and me: then broke
The thunder like a whole sea overhead—

The exquisitely simple song of Pippa breaks in on their passion:

The year's at the spring,
And day's at the morn;
Morning's at seven;
The hill-side's dew-pearled;
The lark's on the wing;
The snail's on the thorn,
God's in his heaven,
All's right with the world.

Strange that the last two lines of this poem, by no means one of Browning's greatest or most significant, are answerable for the widespread misconception of him as the inveterate optimist. That "God's in his heaven"—taking the word heaven in its widest meanings—he certainly never doubted, but to assert that he found "all right with the world" would be an absurd statement. He was too much the realist, as every great poet is, to hold any such view. Like all profound thinkers, his judgments were elastic, while the groundwork of his philosophy remained inflexible.

Throughout *Pippa Passes* the influence of nature is strong: references to sunsets, the morning star, swallows, insects, the cuckoo, flowers and trees.

In Luigi's dialogue with his mother, certain aspects of nature appear to have a definite influence on his projects:

MOTHER: Why go to-night?
Morn's for adventure. Jupiter is now
A morning star. . . .
LUIGI: "I am the bright and morning star," saith God—
And "to such an one I give the morning-star."
The gift of the morning-star! Have I God's gift
Of the morning-star?
MOTHER: Chiara will love to see
That Jupiter an evening-star next June.
LUIGI: True, Mother. Well for those who live through June!
Great noon-tides, thunder-storms, all glaring pomps
That triumph at the heels of June the god
Leading his revel through the leafy world. . . .

Then there is the lovely passage echoing again the thought "There shall never be one lost good":

. . . Last night's sunsets, and great stars
That had a right to come first and see ebb
The crimson wave that drifts the sun away—
Those crescent moons with notched and burning rims
That strengthened into sharp fire, and there stood
Impatient of the azure—and that day
In March, a double rainbow stopped the storm—
May's warm slow yellow moonlit nights—
Gone are they, but I have them in my soul!

Here the vivid sense of the quality of certain months is brilliantly conveyed. There is in all poetry, in all strongly imaginative writing, a mystery: the words become charged with the writer's emotion, not by the use of qualifying adjectives or adverbs, or by elaborate, skilled and purposeful phrasing, but by the "passion and the life" behind them. This incarnation is, and will doubtless remain, a mystery; creative suffering is perhaps the clue. "A man must himself be deeply moved before he is able to move others."

Garden Fancies, "The Flower's Name," is a delicious short poem: a picture of a garden, and the lady of the garden, her spirit infusing the loveliness around her, her own loveliness increased by the surrounding beauty: a divine reciprocity, as in love, when the lover gains strength and capacity for giving more and more love from the emotion that gives so richly to him and is itself mysteriously enriched thereby.

The use of adjectives in *Meeting at Night* is masterly: the words chosen in themselves commonplace, yet conveying precisely the feeling of the night by the sea. "The *long* black land," "the half-moon large and low," "the *startled* little waves," "the pushing prow" of the boat. But here is the complete vivid picture:

> The grey sea and the long black land;
> And the yellow half-moon large and low;
> The startled little waves that leap

In fiery ringlets from their sleep
As I gain the cove with pushing prow,
And quench its speed in the slushy sand.

Then the next morning: (*Parting at Morning*)

Round the cape of a sudden came the sea,
And the sun looked over the mountain's rim.

Few words, and so much said. A lesser poet would have written line after photographic line.

Again, in *A Lover's Quarrel*, it is interesting to observe the economy of diction, another typically modern characteristic:

Oh, what a dawn of day!
How the March wind feels like May,
All is blue again
After last night's rain,
And the South dries the hawthorn-spray.
Only, my Love's away!
I'd as lief that the blue were grey.

Runnels, which rillets swell,
Must be dancing down the dell,
With a foaming head
On the beryl bed
Paven smooth as a hermit's cell;
Each with a tale to tell,
Could my Love but attend as well. . . .

This poem is shot through with the lover's emotion, colouring for him the whole natural world; nature's beauty and poignancy aggravating his suffering:

Here's the spring back or close,
When the almond-blossom blows;
We shall have the word
In a minor third
There is none but the cuckoo knows:
Heaps of the guelder-rose!
I must bear with it, I suppose.

Could but November come,
Were the noisy birds struck dumb. . . .

Tormented as he is, the desire possesses him that nature should in some way accord with his mood, rather than seem to mock at it with indifference, or with a heartless aloof beauty he cannot bear. This reaction to natural beauty is common. He has not learned, indeed, may never learn, the faculty of detachment which, for the creative artist at all events, becomes a necessity so urgent that unless he attains to it, life is no longer possible. As the years pass, every aspect of nature becomes so pregnant with associations, the relentless procession of the seasons brings with it so heavy a burden of memory and thought that the man of acute sensibility must find some way of escape, or die. There is only one solution: to "give beauty back to God, beauty's self and beauty's giver," [1] and so free it of the intolerable entanglement

[1] Gerard Manley Hopkins, *The Leaden Echo and The Golden Echo.*

with human emotion. Nature's beauty transcends human sentiments; man has done wrong to belittle it by identifying it with his own passions, colouring it perpetually with his own thoughts; it is a subtle desecration which brings its own punishment. The faculty of detachment is a primary essential in all creative processes; not until emotion is purged of its personal element is the artist free to create a work of value. The personal emotion must have been there in the first place, of course, but a long and involved process has to work itself out before the necessary creative freedom is attained.

The justly famous poem *Home Thoughts from Abroad* is innocent of human emotion as human; it throbs with the purged passion for nature's beauty alone. There is a similar difference between the love of nature for its own sake and love of it for emotional associative reasons as there is between divine and human love. The poem is too beautiful not to quote in full:

> Oh, to be in England
> Now that April's there,
> And whoever wakes in England
> Sees, some morning, unaware,
> That the lowest boughs and the brushwood sheaf
> Round the elm-tree bole are in tiny leaf,
> While the chaffinch sings on the orchard bough
> In England—now!

And after April, when May follows,
And the whitethroat builds, and all the swallows!
Hark, where my blossomed pear-tree in the hedge
Leans to the field and scatters on the clover
Blossoms and dew-drops—at the bent spray's edge—
That's the wise thrush; he sings each song twice over
Lest you should think he never could recapture
The first fine careless rapture!
And though the fields look rough with hoary dew,
All will be gay when noontide wakes anew
The buttercups, the little children's dower
—Far brighter than this gaudy melon-flower!

This is the kind of poem of England that could only be written in exile. As often in human relationships, distance is necessary to give the true perspective; proximity tends to blur the image.

The nature-writing in *Saul*, as in *Sordello*, is entirely in harmony with the whole quality of the poem. For example:

Have ye seen when Spring's arrowy summons goes
 straight to the aim,
And some mountain, the last to withstand her, that held
 (he alone
While the vale laughed in freedom and flowers) on a broad
 bust of stone
A year's snow bound about for a breast-plate,—leaves
 grasp of the sheet,
Fold on fold all at once it crowds thunderously down to
 his feet,

And there fronts you, stark, black, but alive yet, your mountain of old,
With his rents, the successive bequeathings of ages untold—
Yea, each harm got in fighting your battles, each furrow and scar
Of his head thrust 'twixt you and the tempest—all hail, there they are! —
Now again to be softened with verdure, again hold the nest
Of the dove, tempt the goat and its young to the green on his crest
For their food in the ardours of summer.

Saul is a poem of strength and of tenderness; both are implicit in this passage. The living pictures of Saul himself are interspersed with nature-imagery:

Death was past, life not come: so he waited. Awhile his right hand
Held the brow, helped the eyes left too vacant forthwith, to remand
To their place what new objects should enter: 'twas Saul as before.
I looked up and dared gaze at those eyes, nor was hurt any more
Than by slow pallid sunsets in autumn, ye watch from the shore,
At their sad level gaze o'er the ocean—a sun's slow decline
Over hills which, resolved in stern silence, o'erlap and entwine
Base with base to knit strength more intensely: so, arm folded arm
O'er the chest whose slow heavings subsided.

Earlier in the poem there is the poignant serpent-image:

He stood as erect as that tent-prop, both arms stretched out
wide
On the great cross-support in the centre, that goes to each
side;
He relaxed not a muscle, but hung there, as, caught in his
pangs
And waiting his change, the king-serpent all heavily hangs,
Far away from his kind, in the pine, till deliverance come
With the spring-time,—so agonized Saul, drear and stark,
blind and dumb.

There could be no more vivid description of Saul's mental and spiritual death-in-life. This poem is perhaps the most poignant analysis of a psychological condition Browning ever wrote. Every detail of the living death, the descent into hell, is acutely apprehended and conveyed, and brilliantly contrasted with the joy and intensity of life-consciousness vibrating through young David. And everywhere in nature David sees God:

In the star, in the stone, in the flesh, in the soul and the
clod,
And thus looking within and around me, I ever renew
(With that stoop of the soul which in bending upraises
it too)
The submission of man's nothing-perfect to God's
all-complete,
As by each new obeisance in spirit I climb to his feet.

Finally, all nature is afire with the wonder of his experience:

> There were witnesses, cohorts about me, to left and to right,
> Angels, powers, the unuttered unseen, the alive, the aware. . . .
>
> . . . .
>
> And the stars of night beat with emotion, and tingled and shot
> Out in fire the strong pain of pent knowledge, but I fainted not,
> For the Hand still impelled me at once, and supported, suppressed
> All the tumult, and quenched it with quiet, and holy behest,
> Till the rapture was shut in itself, and the earth sank to rest.

Here nature need not remain unclouded by man's emotion, for David's great task, though emotional, though human, by virtue of the quality of his love for Saul, is yet transcendent, for it has involved the saving of a soul for God, and at such times it is easy to believe that the whole natural world may hold its breath, and later rejoice at the result.

In *By the Fireside* there is a definite suggestion that nature can play a part in man's destiny:

> The lights and the shades made up a spell
> Till the trouble grew and stirred.

Yet in these great moments, as in all vital human experience, it is as if no single factor were responsible, but rather that each part contributes inevitably to the whole. There are certain periods in life when all seems converging on one focal point: innumerable small occurrences combine to build up the final crisis; later, in retrospect, the inevitability of each incident is clear.

> The forests had done it; there they stood;
> We caught for a moment the powers at play:
> They had mingled us so, for once and good,
> Their work was done—might go or stay,
> They relapsed to their ancient mood.

If indeed it were so, if "the powers at play" had taken a hand in the human drama, then a certain power had drawn the lovers to that spot at that time; there was no possibility of escape. Such a belief suggests an answer to the problem of predestination and free-will. If God has a plan for each individual life, the issue is decided, there is no alternative. But—and this is the important factor—the individual is of course unaware of the plan, therefore his will is *apparently* "free."[1] He cannot know that the issue is decided, so has always the *illusion* of choice. In retrospect, how-

[1] The eighteenth-century philosopher Galiani held this view: "Man, therefore, is free because he is intimately persuaded that he is, and this state of mind has exactly the same value as freedom itself." See *The Passions of Life* by William Romaine Paterson, pp. 104–105.

ever, the realization that there has really been no "choice" emerges. "It was ordained to be so." For the Christian holding this belief there is a calm in chaos impossible to the faithless:

> If this counsel or this work be of men, it will come to nought: but if it be of God, ye cannot overthrow it.[1]

"My times be in thy hand." There is no need to struggle, to question, to fear. "Take no thought for the morrow," for "all things work together for good to them that love God." Acceptance, endurance and faith are the watchwords of the Christian when all seems dark and confusing, for the "finger of God, the flash of the Will that can" is seen in everything.

In *By the Fireside*, nature is clearly regarded as a divine agent:

> . . . Hands unseen
> Were hanging the night around us fast;
> But we knew that a bar was broken between
> Life and life: we were mixed at last
> In spite of the mortal screen.
>
> . . . .
>
> How the world is made for each of us!
> How all we perceive and know in it
> Tends to some moment's product thus,
> When a soul declares itself—to wit,
> By its fruit, the thing it does!

[1] *Acts of the Apostles* v. 38–39.

Be hate that fruit or love that fruit,
It forwards the general deed of man,
And each of the Many helps to recruit
The life of the race by the general plan. . . .

. . . .

I am named and known by that moment's feat;
There took my station and degree;
So grew my own small life complete. . . .

. . . .

So the earth has gained by one man more,
And the gain of earth must be Heaven's gain too. . .

He has not missed his great chance, as so many of Browning's characters do, and here again we observe Browning's pre-eminent belief in the necessity to seize the vital moment, in the cause of the soul's true development. And this is linked up with the Christian view of the ultimate redemption of humanity through a change of heart in each individual. The vital moment so continually stressed by Browning is the great test, and so long as the life has been lived for God, and not for selfish ends, there cannot be a failure, or a false decision: the outcome of the crisis must in some way "forward the general deed of man." The egotist will inevitably fail. Here, again, the Christian ideal of selflessness is the practical ideal, the only true solution. But selflessness is not an ideal to be aimed at consciously; like the Kingdom of Heaven, it comes "not with observation," but as a by-product of the surrender of the will to God. Spiritual values, though always to be desired, must not be directly sought, or anxiously pursued:

> Only to those who watch and wait, with absolute indifference to the season of revelation, do all things reveal themselves.

Man's impatience is contrary to the laws of nature, which know nothing of haste. To be sufficiently awake and aware to recognize the vital moment when it comes presupposes long and rigorous training in the pursuit of truth.

The scene of *By the Fireside* is suitably set in autumn, for it is a calm, mature poem, all glowing colour, warmth and peace, retrospective and wise.

> . . . If I tread
> This path back, is it not in pride
> To think how little I dreamed it led
> To an age so blest that, by its side,
> Youth seems the waste instead?

Because he is happy, the "path back," fatal path for the unhappy, is safe to tread, and he rejoices in recalling every moment in the woods so many autumns ago, the November afternoon that preluded all his later happiness. The lovely autumn pictures are exquisitely woven in with his thoughts:

Oh, the sense of the yellow mountain-flowers,
And thorny balls, each three in one,
The chestnuts throw on our path in showers!
For the drop of the woodland-fruit's begun,
These early November hours.

That crimson the creeper's leaf across
Like a splash of blood, intense, abrupt,
O'er a shield else gold from rim to boss,
And lay it for show on the fairy-cupped
Elf-needled mat of moss.

Then there are the "rose-flesh mushrooms, undivulged last evening," the "stagnant pond, danced over by the midge," the ruined chapel, chapel and bridge "of stone alike, blackish-grey and mostly wet," the "boulder-stones where lichens mock the marks on a moth," small ferns "fitting their teeth to the polished block." "The place is silent, *and aware*"—here, again, the conviction that nature had its part to play in the drama. Then the lovely lines:

The water slips o'er stock and stone;
The West is tender, hardly bright:
How grey at once is the evening grown—
One star, the chrysolite!

They have crossed the crumbling bridge in silence, looked at the chapel; his heart "convulsed to really speak, lay choking in its pride." Then in one infinite moment, the woodland spell, the whole scene, the sights and sounds, lights and shades, compelled him to take the chance to "make the little much," to "gain a lover and lose a friend," prepared to "taste a very hell on earth for the hope of such a prize." . . ."The forests had done it."

In *Two in the Campagna* also, the powerful sense of nature's beauty and significance is integral to the lover's mood:

> The champaign with its endless fleece
> Of feathery grasses everywhere!
> Silence and passion, joy and peace,
> An everlasting wash of air—
> Rome's ghost since her decease.
>
> Such life there, through such lengths of hours,
> Such miracles performed in play,
> Such primal naked forms of flowers,
> Such letting nature have her way,
> While heaven looks from its towers!

So he cries:

> Let us be unashamed of soul,
> As earth lies bare to heaven above!
> How it it under our control
> To love or not to love?

But the peace of the Roman campagna is not in his heart; the subtly frustrated lover discerns only, through the lack in his own life, "infinite passion, and the pain of finite hearts that yearn." Like *Andrea del*

Sarto, this poem reveals a most delicate and subtle tragedy of love. The lover is caught in a trap from which there is no escape: there is no tangible situation to deal with, no valid reason why he should desire to escape: to all outward appearances he is content, successful, and attempting to grasp at the full meaning of the strange emotional entanglement, he finds himself clutching at shadows without substance or form, and is left empty-handed and dismayed. He knows he cannot endure it, but what exactly is it that is so unendurable? Simply that the object of his love lacks the capacity to be "all to him," is "just so much, no more," and this is no one's fault, no one is to blame for these tragedies of incompatibility. It was this tragedy, however, that killed Keats. There is a love that leads to life, and a love that leads to death, either psychic or actual. The human mind revolts at certain emotional disasters, which have no more substance than a cloud, and like a cloud envelop, enshroud and suffocate. It remains for a new kind of psycho-physical science to discover what proportion of physical illness has its origin in emotional tragedy. When this kind of investigation is undertaken, the results will be startling.[1]

One of Browning's loveliest poems, *In a Gondola*, is full of exquisite pictures of Venice by night, and

[1] Neither psycho-therapy nor spiritual healing has at present precisely the right approach.

again the sense of the scene intensified and beautified by the emotion of the lovers:

> I send my heart up to thee, all my heart
> In this my singing,
> For the stars help me, and the sea bears part;
> The very night is clinging
> Closer to Venice' streets to leave me space
> Above me, whence thy face
> May light my joyous heart to thee its dwelling-place.
>
> . . . .
>
> Oh, which were best, to roam or rest?
> The land's lap, or the water's breast?
> To sleep on yellow millet-sheaves,
> Or swim in lucid shallows just
> Eluding water-lily leaves. . . .?

There are delicate references to the moth and the bee, and the stanza where the lover pictures the lady transcendent:

> Lie back: could thought of mine improve you?
> From this shoulder let there spring
> A wing; from this, another wing;
> Wings, not legs and feet, shall move you!
> Snow-white must they spring, to blend
> With your flesh, but I intend
> They shall deepen to the end,
> Broader, into burning gold,
> Till both wings crescent-wise enfold
> Your perfect self, from 'neath your feet
> To o'er your head, where, lo, they meet
> As if a million sword-blades hurled
> Defiance from you to the world!

Here, again, is the sense of flesh irradiated by soul, so frequent in Browning's love-poetry. "Earth had attained to heaven, there was no more near or far." Browning was no friend to a philosophy which condemns matter, and asserts that spirit cannot be manifested through so gross a medium. Both body and spirit are equally part of God's earthly plan, and love-sight discloses in a flash the essential unity of apparently conflicting elements, although the lover, like the mystic, is unable to describe in exact words the nature of the vision. He only knows that all life contributes to the momentary flash of understanding:

> The stars help me, and the sea bears part,
> The very night is clinging
> Closer to Venice' streets. . . .

He lives, despite danger, in a friendly universe.

The later poems of Browning may lack to a certain extent the pure lyrical quality in nature-writing, but the power increases, as, for instance, in the magnificent description of the sunset in *Fifine at the Fair*. Throughout Browning's life, love and power alternated, interpenetrated, in his mind as supreme values; in his nature-writing he continually reveals both.

CHAPTER IV

THE POET OF CHRISTIANITY

. . . dispensed
From seeking to be influenced
By all the less immediate ways
That earth, in worships manifold,
Adopts to reach, by prayer and praise,
The garment's hem, which, lo, I hold!

—*Christmas Eve.*

NO other English poet is so consistently and continuously the Christian as Browning. His Christianity was not a religion superimposed on his personality; in a very real sense, it *was* his personality. His life was quite literally given to God. And yet he is not regarded as a devotional, poet, in the sense that George Herbert is, or Crashaw, Vaughan, Alice Meynell or Francis Thompson. A certain indefinable breadth of outlook, a grandeur, freedom, sanity, in short, "wholeness," in his personality excludes him from narrow categories. A comparison with Gerard Manley Hopkins here suggests itself. Hopkins, although perhaps the most religious of all poets, cannot be called devotional, either. His work in some curious way transcends the devotional, because in his case also his religion was his life: every word he wrote was suffused with a sense of God and the eternal; he could not write anything that was divorced from his faith, because his faith was himself.

There is a profound significance in the words at the beginning of St. John's Gospel:

> He came unto His own, and His own received Him not. But as many as received Him, to them gave He power to become the sons of God, even to them that believe on His name:
>
> Which were born, not of blood, nor of the will of the flesh, nor of the will of man, but of God.

Mr. Merezhkovsky in *The Secret of the West* suggests that certain beings are born of man and woman "and of something else besides." These are God's ordained messengers on earth: the prophets, the saints, the great poets. And this, in the case of Browning, accounts for his independence in matters of religion: it was not possible for him to submit to any particular sect; truth was in all, yet absolute and final truth in none, because, in all, truth is obscured in one way or another by man-imposed doctrine. Jesus said: "None cometh unto the Father but by Me." This is the inevitable belief of the religious genius: Christ only, Christ always, points the way to God; there are no intermediaries. Through the miracle of the Incarnation, God became accessible to man, and in Christ there is direct communion with God, a relationship otherwise impossible, since no man can see God and live. But to see Jesus Christ is to be admitted into fullness of life.

It is of this experience that Browning writes in *Christmas Eve:* the vision of Christ, the truth, in the midst of a myriad conflicting aspects of truth presented in the chapel, St. Peter's in Rome, and the lecture-hall. Unfortunately this magnificent poem is marred here and there by the extraordinary rhyming-devices that afflict Browning from time to time. In a poem as grave and momentous as this, the fault is especially unfortunate, and the thought inevitably occurs that the measured tread of blank verse would have been more suitable to the subject. The peculiar rhyming and the rather rollicking metre of the poem cannot be other than inharmonious. But this is mere technical carping: the essence of the work is unaffected, and it remains one of the greatest of Browning's religious poems, giving a clear view of his fundamental religious beliefs. "Love is the ever-springing fountain." This is the basis of his faith. God is love, and the concept of love—taking the word in its widest meanings—is recurrent in all Browning's poetry. In *Paracelsus*, for example, the poet Aprile desires to "love infinitely," through love he knows he will reach what Paracelsus seeks through knowledge, and

> . . . all poets, God ever meant
> Should save the world, and therefore lent
> Great gifts to. . . .

Poets are given pre-eminently God's great gift of love:

Love which endures and doubts and is oppressed
And cherished, suffering much and much sustained,
And blind, oft-failing, yet believing love,
A half-enlightened, often-chequered trust:—
Hints and previsions of which faculties,
Are strewn confusedly everywhere about
The inferior natures, and all lead up higher,
All shape out dimly the superior race,
The heir of hopes too fair to turn out false.

Every kind of love is glorious, of inestimable value to development:

PARACELSUS: And I know you, dearest Festus!
And how you love unworthily; and how
All admiration renders blind.
FESTUS: You hold that admiration blinds?
PARACELSUS: Ay and alas!
FESTUS: Nought blinds you less than admiration, friend!
Whether it be that all love renders wise
In its degree; from love which blends with love—
Heart answering heart—to love which spends itself
In silent mad idolatry of some
Pre-eminent mortal, some great soul of souls,
Which ne'er will know how much it is adored.
I say, such love is never blind.

This love, often slightingly dismissed as "idealistic" and therefore "unreal," is, in fact, the love that leads to the stars, for it is the love of the ideal manifested in the individual, nothing less than the image of God reflected in a human form. In this love human and divine are perfectly blended. Again the lines from *Abt Vogler* are apposite:

> And the emulous heaven yearned down, made effort to reach the earth
> As the earth had done her best, in my passion, to reach the sky.

Both great love and great art effect the marriage of heaven and earth. The concept of ideal love is inborn: hence the child's tendency to hero-worship and identification. Almost all subsequent misfortunes in later life are due to the destruction of this ideal.

Paracelsus realizes that Aprile's capacity for love leads him nearer to truth than all his knowledge. Aprile has found beauty, he, power. But it has never been said that power is truth, whereas beauty, goodness and truth are one. Even at the outset—Browning was only twenty-three when he wrote *Paracelsus*—he knew love was predominant:

> . . . love preceding
> Power, and with much power, always much more love;
> Love still too straitened in his present means,
> And earnest for new power to set it free.

So throughout his poetry love is the supreme value. "Too much love there can never be"; that is the conclusion in *Christmas Eve*, and the lines from *A Soul's Tragedy* beginning "my soul's capacity for love widens" proclaim his understanding of the full meaning of love: the universal love apprehended so clearly always by the poets, philosophers and saints, and in life so tragically misunderstood. In *Pippa Passes* and in *Saul* the ideal of love is interwoven with the ideal of service: again a Christian concept. It is Pippa's love that has given her the power she does not know she possesses, so that her mere passing, the mere sound of her voice, turns human hearts. Wholly ignorant that she has this power, she reflects at the day's end:

> Now, one thing I should like to really know:
> How near I ever might approach all these. . . .
>
> . . . .
>
> Approach, I mean, so as to touch them, so
> As to . . . in some way . . . move them—if you please,
> Do good or evil to them some slight way. . . .
>
> . . . .
>
> God bless me! I can pray no more to-night.
> No doubt, some way or other, hymns say right,
> "All service ranks the same with God—
> With God, whose puppets, best or worst
> Are we: there is no last nor first."

She can never know how dramatic her passing has been. God does not show immediate results, nor does the true Christian ask for them to be shown: the love, and the service for God, the knowledge of the motive, is enough. Filled wholly with love of life, and of human beings as a vivid and essential part of life, happy in her faith, Pippa cannot choose but serve, yet, like the wise artist, she does not set out to change human hearts; it is her own beauty of soul, her own all-embracing love, that works the miracle; there is no striving, no evangelizing; she loves God, and all God's children. The result is inevitable. "Be ye perfect . . ."; that behest is the key that unlocks the door to the Kingdom of Heaven:

> We all, with unveiled face reflecting as a mirror the glory of the Lord, are transformed into the same image from glory to glory. . . .[1]

But the mirror must be without blemish. Persistently, ceaselessly, the world, ruled by the Prince of Darkness, strives to overthrow the power of love, which is the manifestation of God on earth. It is the eternal battle of "Michael and his angels going forth to war with the dragon."[2] The moment God (Love) enters and takes possession of the soul, the warfare begins:

> The devil tempteth not unbelievers and sinners, whom he has already in secure possession; but the faithful and devout he tempts and harasses in many ways.[3]

[1] 2 *Corinthians* iii. 18.
[2] *Revelation* xii. 7.
[3] Thomas à Kempis, *The Imitation of Christ*.

The vital necessity is to recognize the nature of the struggle; thus forewarned, the soul is to a certain extent forearmed. Only full recognition of the devil can outwit him; it is useless to turn and run with closed eyes from the problem of evil, hopefully doubting its true existence, and so trusting not to be overtaken. St. George did not kill the dragon by disbelieving in its reality. There are too many references in Jesus's own words to be able to doubt the reality of the Evil One.

Professor Grabo in his interesting book on the growth of Shelley's thought, *The Magic Plant*, stresses Shelley's early disillusionment with human nature:

> He learned reality[1] far more rapidly than most and very early freed himself from sentimentality and false illusions.

It soon became clear to him that his forceful efforts at reform were useless: the failure of the Irish experiment began the disillusionment. The ideals and ideas outlined in his *Address to the Irish People* are eminently reasonable and necessary; many have since been adopted, and many more will have to be before very long, if civilization is to be saved, but neither the address nor his journey to Ireland to attempt to convert the people met with any success. It was not

[1] The word "reality" appears to be used here as meaning "actuality", not reality in the philosophic sense.

long before he realized that he must abandon direct methods and work for the evil world by means of his art only. Action only led to tragic misunderstanding, and often disaster. Shelley's attitude to human problems and his reactions to abuse and malevolence prove him in essence, if not technically, a saint. Such men are peculiarly endowed with the capacity to understand and reflect God's power of love: hence their persecution. There is no danger of permanent damage, the work will be done, yet the prophet can be temporarily hindered by the poison of relationships that have from time to time the power to blur the mirror. This was continually Shelley's misfortune. He was dogged throughout his life by poisoning human contacts; yet in spite of every setback and disaster, his work continued. No earthly power can overthrow God's purposes. It will never be conceded by the mass that certain individuals have knowledge that is hidden from other men. Even so enlightened a woman as Julia Wedgwood ventured to argue with Browning about his attitude to good and evil as he unfolded it in *The Ring and the Book*.[1] As usual, the prophet was without honour in his own country. A clearer vision would have shown her why the God-given friendship was at last taken from her: she should have trodden more circumspectly on holy ground.

[1] *Robert Browning and Julia Wedgwood.* A Broken Friendship as revealed in their Letters.

But "only he who sees takes off his shoes." A poet of Browning's spiritual stature is not to be argued with: the proper attitude is reverence, humility, and a desire to understand, as far as possible, the truths that have been shown to him alone, and which he finds only too hard to expound. This difficulty, allied to his unassailable certainty, his claim to "know," lays him open often to the charge of dogmatism; whereas the fact is that his paradoxical position—certainty of the revealed truth, and uncertainty of his own power to make it clear—actually produces a state of mind the reverse of dogmatic. The appearance of absolute conviction is unconscious compensation for his confusing sense of certainty and insecurity. And he is handicapped at the outset by being un-at-home in the world. So Jesus, wisest of poets, spoke in parables. "Who hath ears to hear, let him hear." He expounded his meaning only to those who were by nature fitted to understand: his chosen disciples. Any other method of revealing spiritual truths can only lead to confusion, and often disaster:

> It requires wisdom to understand wisdom; the music is nothing if the audience is deaf.[1]

As Professor Wilson Knight, in his chapter on "The Prophetic Imagination" in *The Christian Renaissance*, points out, Jesus

[1] Walter Lippmann, *A Preface to Morals.*

finds the same difficulty, as anyone must who works from an imaginative centre, in explaining his message to those whose minds work differently.

He, being divine, overcame this difficulty by parable-speech; the poet and the prophet, being human, still grieve at the deafness of the audience, are still tempted sometimes to strive by patient argument to reveal truth, especially if their silence runs the risk of inflicting hurt where none should ever be inflicted, which accounts for Browning's own attempt at explanation in the misunderstanding about *The Ring and the Book*. He felt a deep love for Julia Wedgwood, and he was too great a Christian to risk hurting her. But the poet's love is not easy to understand, and impossible to analyse. It is personal and super-personal, in the same sense that poetry itself is. Eros and Psyche are bound in so close a union that they find contact with the outside world difficult. Browning "loved" Julia Wedgwood, but to analyse the quality and full meaning of that love is beyond the power of "average conscientious intelligent opinion" (to borrow Mr. Michael Roberts's valuable phrase) which can only understand those things which lie within the measure of its own mental and spiritual development. It naturally follows that many unwise things have been written and said of this newly-discovered relationship in Browning's life. It should be realized that the psychology of the artist requires special study, and an unusual degree of perception. Beatrice Hinkle, in *The Recreating of the Individual*, writes well on this subject, stating facts already abundantly clear to the artist himself, but shrouded in perplexity for others. She says:

> The true artist has always been and still is a being somewhat apart from the rest of humanity, and is entitled to be considered in a class by himself. . . . He . . . possesses a reality of a different order from that of the ordinary man. His ego is entirely identified with his creative processes which for him constitute the entire meaning and purpose of his life.

"The *entire* meaning and purpose of his life." All other activities, relationships, problems, are subsidiary to this purpose, or are in some way feeding it, otherwise they must be abandoned. Certainly it is vitally necessary to render powerless any situation or relationship that threatens the life of the creative ego. The poet's conception of love, and the relations of the sexes, accounts for the otherwise inexplicable friendships, in which the love-element is not excluded—indeed, must not be, since this is the element most intimately linked up with creativeness—but is never allowed to assume absolute sovereignty. The artist and the saint know the meaning of the words: "neither bond nor free, neither male nor female";[1] they only, by virtue of their full understanding of sex as a part of life, and

[1] *Galatians* iii. 28.

not life itself, are finally capable of attaining to a sexless love wherein sex is not excluded but sublimated. The pure in heart not only see God: they see human beings as God's children, not as creatures sharply divided into opposite sexes. This ultimate ideal, in essence entirely different from what is usually meant by "sex-equality," was expressed by Shelley in the lines from *The Revolt of Islam:*

> Never will peace and human nature meet
> Till free and equal man and woman greet
> Domestic peace. . . .

In recent years, the science of psycho-analysis has ludicrously overstressed the importance of sex in human life. Those wiser than the scientists know that there is only one true life-centre, and that to attribute every human ill and maladjustment to a single primary cause is to overlook the real core of the malady. Psycho-analysis prescribes palliatives, and unless the readjusted life is founded on a basis more substantial than an understanding of mental processes—vitally important knowledge but not the final wisdom—eventually there will be shipwreck again.

There is an interesting reference to the power of evil in the *Old Testament* story of King Saul and David:

> Now the spirit of the Lord departed from Saul, and an evil spirit from the Lord troubled him.

This rouses many involved speculations, coinciding exactly with Luther's pronouncement that the devil was "God's devil," used by God for His own ends. In *Cristina* Browning writes:

> Never fear but there's provision
> Of the devil's to quench knowledge
> Lest we walk the earth in rapture!

and continues:

> Making those who catch God's secret
> Just so much more prize their capture.

Which seems to suggest again that the devil's provision to quench knowledge is in itself a part of God's plan. But in spite of all he wrote on good and evil, and the baffling problem of evil in God's good world, it would be impossible to assert that Browning gave any final answer. Indeed, being human, how could he? He wrote in one of his letters to Julia Wedgwood:

> I like *knowing* at any price. It is a heavy price sometimes, leaving us penniless. Yet it is a good bargain.

In writing *The Ring and the Book* he would not evade any issues. Truth must always come first, and there the truth included much evil. "This is God's world, as he made it for reasons of his own," he wrote, again to Julia Wedgwood. It was not his business to account for the reasons. If, in telling the story of Guido, Pompilia and Caponsacchi, the evil in Guido made the good in Pompilia and Caponsacchi shine out more brilliantly, so much the better, but this was not Browning's intention in writing the poem. No great poet would embark on a work with any such "intention." Intentions, indeed, are always far enough from the poet's conscious mind. There is only one reason why he writes poetry: because he must.

In *Saul* the fight between good and evil is a comparatively plain issue. The Old Testament story clearly stresses God's plan:

> And it came to pass, when the evil spirit from God was upon Saul, that David took the harp, and played with his hand: so Saul was refreshed, and was well, and the evil spirit departed from him.

David's love for Saul is as much the love of God as any purely personal emotion:

> And oh, all my heart how it loved him! but where was the sign?
> I yearned—"Could I help thee, my father, inventing a bliss,
> I would add, to that life of the past, both the future and this;
> I would give thee new life altogether, as good, ages hence
> As this moment—had love but the warrant, love's heart to dispense!"

"I would give thee new life altogether"—the cry of passionate compassionate love, the agony of desire to save a human soul. And the intensity of this selfless love, the pure love of friendship and service in God's cause, gave David the power he yearned for: "Then the truth came upon me," till in the last words of his impassioned speech he pours out the prophecy of the coming of the greatest consoler:

> . . . O Saul, it shall be
> A Face like my face that receives thee: a Man like to me,
> Thou shalt love and be loved by, for ever: a Hand like this hand
> Shall throw open the gates of new life to thee! See the Christ stand!

David's love for Saul was passionate prayer, and his prayer was answered, because he was aware throughout that only God's power working through him could save Saul; he had no faith in himself alone, only in himself as God's servant to

> . . . save and redeem and restore him, maintain at the height
> This perfection—succeed with life's dayspring death's minute of night. . . .
> Interpose at the difficult minute, snatch Saul, the mistake,
> Saul, the failure, the ruin he seems now,—and bid him awake
> From the dream, the probation, the prelude, to find himself set
> Clear and safe in new light and new life,—a new harmony yet
> To be run, and continued, and ended—who knows?—or endure!

The whole poem throbs with David's compassionate desire. His manner of helping Saul is a perfect example of Christian psychology: he suffers with the sufferer without losing his own strength, sees and understands the root of the pain, yet never emits one word of reproach or suggests any direct means of escape from it; pins all his faith on the power of God to heal; knows that God, in using him, will show him the best way to guide Saul back to sanity and health. Everything about his technique is positive, constructive; there are no regrets, no sentimental groanings with the sufferer; all his activities are directed towards the positive good of recovery. Sympathy alone can be a form of sentimentality, a weak indulgence in the contemplation of suffering which is really in essence self-pity; without constructive thought and action it has no root in reality. Browning was one of the greatest of Christian psychologists, though he worked before psychotherapy as a science was heard of.

From *Saul* to *Caliban upon Setebos* is a far cry, both in matter and in manner, yet *Caliban* is almost equally a poem of immense Christian significance. The speculations of the savage, scarcely human Caliban as to the meaning and purpose of the Universe differ but little in actual fact from much modern questioning. This is where scientific agnostic thought has led us: back to the philosophical position of the savage! The trouble is inevitably the same when the human mind attempts to reduce eternal concepts to temporal terms. Caliban is the typical ego-centric agnostic. "He hath a spite against me," he feels; the Power behind the Universe, whatever it may be, must be propitiated, and it will not be safe to let him think all goes too well with Caliban. "The gods are athirst":

> As flies to wanton boys are we to the gods,—
> They kill us for their sport.[1]

This pagan notion is still prevalent, even among some who call themselves Christians. Clearly, God has a spite against them. The more they try to live the good life—as they conceive it—the more suffering is inflicted on them. God is determined they shall not be happy. This unfortunate view is bound up with the general idea of Christian suffering, a misconception of the meaning of the Cross. And rather naturally; too much stress has been laid on the concept of suffering, as if it were an end in itself, rather than a means to an end. Even so enlightened a Christian thinker as Thomas à Kempis says: "The whole life of Christ was a cross and a martyrdom," how then shall his followers expect to escape continuous suffering? But the Gospels themselves tell no such story. There are scarcely any references to Jesus's sufferings until the Agony in the Garden and the Crucifixion. Occasionally we are told that he "groaned

[1] *King Lear*, Act IV, Sc. 1.

in spirit," that he grieved at the hardness of men's hearts, and certainly he wept at the grave of Lazarus, but it is wrong to stress the idea of his sufferings on earth, rather than his joy. Is it conceivable that the Divine Man, living in perfect union with God, suffered continual pain? Union with God is the supreme aim of the Christian life, and it cannot be true that the one man in history who attained to it on earth knew more pain than joy. No doubt he, either imaginatively or in actual fact, experienced every kind of suffering human life is heir to, but his transcendent knowledge of God and of God's purpose for man shining through every moment of difficulty must have sustained him as no human being has ever yet been sustained.

Caliban's words:

> . . . the best way to escape His ire
> Is, not to seem too happy,

find a reflection in the usual warnings to the young whenever they show signs of extreme joy; they are told they will suffer for it later. Joy, it seems, is not only unnatural and in some way wrong, but dangerous. Such demonstrations of delight tempt Fate. What a criticism of God, Who intends that His chosen people should be joyful. No child should be taught to suspect danger in happiness; it is a blasphemy to quell the fountain that sparkles with divine innocence. The truth is that there is no earthly joy comparable to the joy of the Christian, nor any suffering comparable in depth and richness and creative power. And the innocent joy of the child reflects in truest earthly perfection the crystalline felicity of the children of God.

The ego-centric agnostic suggests that if there is a God at all, He should at least refrain from tormenting *him*. This attitude is the antithesis of the viewpoint of the saint, who lives only to further God's purposes, having no interest in himself except as a servant of God. Whatever God may ask of him, he is content, although often the reason for his sufferings may be temporarily almost impossibly hard to understand:

> I know thee, who hast kept my path, and made
> Light for me in the darkness, tempering sorrow
> So that it reached me like a solemn joy.
> It were too strange that I should doubt thy love.[1]

Professor Hywel Hughes, in his invaluable study *The Philosophic Basis of Mysticism*, writes well of the apparently paradoxical introversion and extraversion of the mystic:

> . . . we may say that the mystic deliberately practises introversion in order that it may make him an extravert in the best sense of the word. . . . He seeks to find himself (through "looking into the sanctuary of his own soul":

[1] *Paracelsus*.

introversion) in order to lose himself in God, but in this "losing his life in God" he finds himself again at a higher and nobler level of being. . . .

Elsewhere I have applied this principle to the artist also:

. . . the ego, while living deeply withdrawn in solitude and silence (*i.e.*, in a state of introversion), yet flows out continually to life (extraversion), giving and gaining, relating every experience to the whole, always trying to piece together the fragments of the pattern, never content with the sensations of the "I" in themselves, but always questioning, searching for the meaning . . . self-preoccupation and concern for development being only the desire to understand how the self may best be used in service to, in the one case (the artist) art, in the other (the saint), God.[1]

Professor Hughes has done a great service to religion by effectively and convincingly exposing the fallacies inherent in the theories of mysticism as psychological abnormality. While freely admitting the apparent similarities, he argues and proves the essential differences, and concludes his argument by an appeal to the *fruits* of the experiences, a point repeatedly stressed by William James in his *Varieties of Religious Experience*. Browning knew nothing of psychology in the modern sense of the word; he died ten years or more before Freud began to publish his investigations into

[1] *Poetry Review*, September–October, 1937.

the processes of the unconscious, but a poet of Browning's stature and scope has certain invaluable information, derived in a different way: his conclusions are "given," not arrived at by scientific research. So it will be found over and over again that his insight into human nature and the obscure workings of the soul is flawless, coinciding startlingly with the latest findings of psychology. Actually, his views are often more balanced than those of many modern psychologists: he never accepts one aspect only of human behaviour as being indicative of a final truth; in the view of the great poets the "nothing-but" theory is untenable; they know there are multitudinous conflicting and bewildering factors governing human motives and actions, and that these factors cannot be reduced to simple terms. The study of psychology is only in its infancy; its immense value is unquestionable, but in its present stage harm is as likely to be done as good, and the dangers to the partly informed can scarcely be over-estimated. Any attempt to simplify human nature can only end in deeper misunderstanding. The study of the human mind is so complex a science—possibly the most complex of all—that only those with exceptional gifts and a unique aptitude should attempt it. Such students will approach the subject with humility and suitable deference, often fearing to tread where so many have rushed in arrogantly. But humility is ever the mark of the great mind. "Something we may see, all we cannot see." It was Browning's task as a poet to reveal life, so far as he could, in its entirety; he knew there were innumerable mental complexities, and mysteries of all kinds, producing the various dramatic situations he portrayed. Somewhere in the morass of confusion the truth lay hidden, and through all the perplexities and sins and torments, the agonies and errors, the one reality shines steadfast, and God is continually revealed, immanent and transcendent. There is scarcely a poem of Browning's in which the name of God does not occur; open the books a hundred times at random, and always it appears, no less in the secular than in the philosophical and religious poems. How indeed could he avoid it? It was as natural for him to talk of God as it was to get up every day and eat his breakfast. This is really the sense in which God exists in the lives of all true Christians. Everything is spontaneously, inevitably, related to the one centre, without thought or effort.

So Browning, continuously preoccupied with thoughts of God and His meaning in all types of human lives, found no more difficulty in writing of Caliban than of the cultured Bishop Blougram. It fascinated him to speculate on the reactions of varying minds to the idea of Deity and the Christian life, and in dozens of poems he pondered on and expanded the theme. No doubt it seemed to him in itself a proof of the existence of God: the fact that no type of mind is wholly insensitive to the idea.

Caliban upon Setebos is the poem of pessimistic theology par excellence; *Bishop Blougram's Apology* puts the practical arguments for Christianity more clearly than any other of Browning's poems. When the Bishop insists:

> My business is not to remake myself,
> But to make the absolute best of what God made. . . .
>
> It is the idea, the feeling and the love,
> God means mankind should strive for and show forth
>
> I act for, talk for, live for this world now,
> As this world prizes action, life and talk,

he speaks as a very practical Christian. Here is no mysticism, in the commonly accepted sense of the word, but the considered pronouncement of a man who has weighed the pros and cons of Christianity in the most practical scales, and finds no alternative but to accept the Christian life as best.

> I have read much, thought much, experienced much . . .
> . . . .
>
> What matter though I doubt at every pore,
> Head-doubts, heart-doubts, doubts at my finger-ends,
> Doubts in the trivial work of every day,
> Doubts at the very bases of my soul
>
> In the grand moments when she probes herself—
> If finally I have a life to show. . . .

I show you doubt to prove that faith exists.

What can I gain on the denying side?

for "Luther gained a real heaven in his heart throughout his life," and this heaven in the heart is the only refuge that makes our difficult existence on earth bearable.

Again, the Bishop's argument here is essentially practical:

> The common problem, yours, mine, everyone's,
> Is, not to fancy what were fair in life
> Provided it could be, but finding first
> What may be, then find out how to make it fair
> Up to our means: a very different thing!

Sound Christian psychology: no wasteful regrets, no grieving on those fatal lines that lead to despair, the vain thoughts of what might have been, no remorse, no idle day-dreaming: life must be accepted courageously as it is, and a worthy edifice built out of the material to hand. The Christian is convinced that the material exactly as it is is the right material; he will not waste time abusing it, nor in complaining that his tools are inefficient; his particular task is to build worthily from what he has, turning each difficulty as it comes into a lesson teaching him to build still better. This is the eminently practical view; never was there so practical a religion as Christianity. The power of Christ can produce in a flash the results for which the psychologist labours often for months, sometimes for years. Psychotherapy is the long and laborious route to soul-health; often, it is true, the only route acceptable, for it is difficult to surrender the whole self to God, the struggle Francis Thompson writes of in *The Hound of Heaven* is usual. It seems unpractical to give life over to an unseen, unknown, often unfelt, power. There is an almost overwhelming sense of fear also, for what is the precise meaning of the words: "Thou shalt have none other gods but Me . . . for I the Lord thy God am a jealous God"? So the poet cries, and many struggling souls echo the cry:

> Yet was I sore adread
> Lest, having Thee, I should have naught beside.

The Hebrew conception of the jealous God, the Lord Jehovah demanding human sacrifice, has done much harm to Christianity, the religion of love. While it is true that God does demand the whole self, and that there can be no genuine spiritual progress until this surrender has been made, there is finally no sense of constraint or loss, but of freedom and infinite gain, and at last the meaning of the words, "My yoke is easy and My burden is light," is fully understood. Like the burden of great human love, this is a burden of treasure which no one who has taken it up would ever lay down again. Yet to the uninitiated the issues seem so confused that reasoning is of no avail. They can only be understood by faith. "You don't believe, you don't and can't," says Bishop Blougram to his guest, "in any revelation called divine." Well, he continues, he himself knows well enough where the difficulties lie which he could not, cannot solve, nor ever will. Never let it be thought that the Christian is ignorant of these problems. But "What's midnight doubt before the day-spring's faith?" and surely: "It's best believing, if we may." . . . "What can I gain on the denying side?" Again, so practical an argument: the way of doubt has nothing to offer but unrest and ultimate despair; the way of belief is the way to peace and positive hope:

> . . . belief's fire, once in us,
> Makes of all else mere stuff to show itself.

But the absolute and final sense of God, "naked belief in God the Omnipotent," the Bishop argues, would be more than our present weakness could bear, "it were the seeing him, no flesh shall dare." So he believes Creation is meant not to reveal God, but to hide him "with shield enough against that sight till we can bear its stress." And he knows that it is when the God-impulse first stirs that the battle between good and evil begins:

> . . . when the fight begins within himself
> A man's worth something. God stoops o'er his head,
> Satan looks up between his feet—both tug—

He's left, himself, in the middle: the soul wakes
And grows. Prolong that battle through his life!
Never leave growing till the life to come!

Life on earth is vitally important, since its use may be to make the next life more intense.

The imagery in the lines just quoted is typically Browningesque. Often his mind took a grotesque twist.

If human life were more commonly looked upon as an education (always Browning's view), the times when the soul is tested could be taken rather in the light of an examination; there would be an ever-springing interest in the development of events, and a sense of wonder, not blind resentment or dumb terror. It would be thrilling to try to see the meaning hidden in the suffering so often seeming cruel and purposeless.

Again, there is a curious typical twist in the fact that at the end of the poem Browning reveals certain unlikeable qualities in Bishop Blougram; indeed, rather more than hints at insincerity. So he shows how much good may come through a character in itself by no means wholly good. Not only the saints are given the power to reveal God, and the unexpected appearance of truth in a welter of falsehood was always a fascinating phenomenon to Browning. Blougram's arguments are no less sound because he "believed, say, half he spoke." The whole poem provides some of

Browning's most powerful reasoning in favour of Christian beliefs. And in the Epilogue to *Dramatis Personæ* he shows that, like Bishop Blougram, he is fully aware of all the anti-Christian arguments, which, however, have for him no shadow of reality. Argument held an irresistible fascination for him; in *La Saisiaz*, for example, he puts forward all the arguments against immortality, in order to refute them. It is this ability to see all sides, this facility comparable with the brilliant pleading and reasoning of the advocate, that gives Browning his unique force as a Christian writer. It must be worth-while to explore the significance of Christianity after considering the powerful arguments of this gigantic mind. He stood firm on his mountain, yet he could always stoop to comfort the struggling sufferers below:

> . . . with that stoop of the soul which in bending upraises it too,[1]

No suffering human being need have hesitated to take his human grief to Browning, for nothing was excluded from his conception of life. A comparison with Shelley suggests itself. It may be possible that Shelley's failure to adjust himself to human life accounted for his tragic associations with human beings. There could be no real contact. He, from his heaven, found it so hard to lean down to reach the

[1] *Saul.*

earth, the tortured earth that filled him with passionate compassion. His home was never there; in this sense Matthew Arnold's sweeping criticism of the "ineffectual angel" is justified. He was as ill at ease in the world as a god who suddenly finds himself among men; the degree of understanding is so far removed that there can be no true sympathy; the immortal sees the folly and the suffering of men, knows the remedy, yet knows not how to adapt his message for human ears, and almost inevitably blunders. But Browning, by virtue of his overmastering sense of true religious values, was well adjusted to life; it was his Christianity that made his compassion constructive. He was the Christian, Shelley more the Deist, and it is the power of Christ, the human God, that gives the human touch. There is no doubt of Browning's wholehearted belief in the words of St. John in *A Death in the Desert:*

> I say, the acknowledgment of God in Christ
> Accepted by thy reason, solves for thee
> All questions in the earth and out of it,

neither is there any doubt that he believed the acceptance *by the reason* to be necessary. There is an interesting Preface to a book on Browning by Edward Berdoe [1] explaining that he was driven to write the book by his sense of a profound debt to Browning, whose poetry rescued him from agnosticism, and

[1] *Browning and the Christian Faith.*

compelled him to believe in the Christian faith as the only religion finally acceptable by the reason. His discovery of Browning's work and the almost immediate conversion is a dramatic story. It happens that the writing of this present book is an attempt to discharge a debt of a rather similar nature. Browning urged "never think of me as dead," and expressed the same thought in the last poem he wrote, the Epilogue to *Asolando*. His wish is fulfilled, for his power, rather than being dimmed by death, has grown, and grows still. It is not possible to think of him as dead. "No work begun shall ever pause for death." Again, he attained to his beliefs. One day we shall no longer look upon death as an end, or even as a disaster. The death of Jesus was no end, but, rather, a glorious beginning. So with the martyrs and the saints, the prophets, the poets. Death is necessary to reveal the full meaning of their lives. It is as if after death the power of the spirit is released to do at last the work life on earth continually hindered.

A Death in the Desert is a very different poem from *Bishop Blougram's Apology*. Here the appeal of the Christian faith has a gentler quality, suitable to a poem concerned with the beloved disciple, the disciple of love. Mr. Sutherland Bates, in one of his interesting notes in *The Bible designed to be Read as Literature*, writes of St. John as the typical Christian mystic to whom the conception of a cleavage between human and divine love was inevitably false. And indeed a thoughtful study of St John's writings should do much to clear away the many misconceptions on a subject usually considered confusing. Every word St. John wrote was saturated with love, the Christian love, Agapé, yet there is nowhere a suggestion that this is the cold love of charity, but everywhere human warmth, compassion, and the understanding that grows only from such love. It transcends while including the personal quality of human love. St. John explains nothing, knowing that there can be no "explanation" of spiritual truth, which can only be apprehended. His words, suffused with emotion, his phrases, radiant and gentle as spring sunlight and as life-giving, convey the quality of his vision. Light and love—the terms are really synonymous—form the keynote of all his writings.

God is light, and in Him is no darkness at all. He that saith he is in the light, and hateth his brother, is in the darkness even until now. He that loveth his brother abideth in the light. . . .

. . . .

He that loveth not abideth in death. . . .

. . . .

Beloved, let us love one another, for love is of God; and everyone that loveth is begotten of God, and knoweth God. He that loveth not knoweth not God, for God is love.

And here is the fundamental principle of Christian psychology:

Perfect love casteth out fear.

Fear is the root-evil in psychological ill-health; it is the driving force behind all suffering and psychic death, and can only be conquered by the other powerful force, love. "He that feareth is not made perfect in love." Fear is death because it is lack of faith in God's power to work miracles in the lives of His children, and only faith is life. "All things work together for good to them that love God," but the life dominated by fear is lived at cross-purposes; because the soul has not been given to God, Satan is in possession instead. There is no compromise in the Christian life. It is because God is love and Satan fear that fear is the supreme enemy to be overcome.

The stress on love and light is as powerful and recurrent in St. John's Gospel as in his Epistles, and in his writings more than in any in the Bible the world is continually referred to as evil, and in direct opposition to the Kingdom of God dwelling in Christ's followers. "The whole world lieth in the hand of the Evil One." No wonder the judgments of the world are evil, and inevitably false. Jesus's long speeches against the world are reported fully only in St. John's Gospel, since only the mystic is fully sensitive to and conscious of the world's blasphemous assaults on love, because only he understands the precise significance of the warfare.

So in *A Death in the Desert* the dying saint continually speaks of the power of love, and says that

. . . truth, deadened of its absolute blaze
Might need love's eye to pierce the outstretched doubt.

He argues from the fact of man's striving ("Man's distinctive mark alone") the proof of his potential perfection. "Man partly is and wholly hopes to be."

> Life, with all it yields of joy and woe,
> And hope and fear—believe the aged friend—
> Is just our chance o' the prize of learning love,
> How love might be, hath been indeed, and is.

God's supreme act of love was the Incarnation.

In St. John's mind there was no difficulty, no need to explain, analyse, dissect or justify the light that irradiated his life. The clue to the open secret, which so many entangle with falsehoods and misconceptions until it seems a mystery, lies in the words "God is love." It follows that the chosen children of God are the children of love: "By this shall all men know that ye are my disciples."

Browning wrote *La Saisiaz*, a long poem on immortality, prompted by the sudden death of a friend, more than thirty years after the dramatic romance *The Flight of the Duchess*. In *La Saisiaz* he argues, rationally examining the whole problem, once again in an easy metre not wholly suited to his subject. The poem is rather in the nature of a disquisition, but there are often lines of great beauty and power:

Only grant my soul may carry high through death her cup unspilled,
Brimming though it be with knowledge, life's loss drop by drop distilled,
I shall boast it mine—the balsam, bless each kindly wrench that wrung
From life's tree its inmost virtue, tapped the root whence pleasure sprung,
Barked the bole, and broke the bough, and bruised the berry, left all grace
Ashes in death's stern alembic, loosed elixir in its place!

It was in *The Flight of the Duchess*, however, that he wrote the true poetry:

And then as, 'mid the dark, a gleam
Of yet another morning breaks,
And like the hand which ends a dream,
Death, with the might of his sunbeam,
Touches the flesh and the soul awakes.

Again and again in *Ferishtah's Fancies* love is honoured as life's supreme value. "Love is praise, and praise is love."

So let us say—not "Since we know, we love,"
But rather "Since we love, we know enough."

Browning is as much the poet of love, romantic love, passionate love, Christian love—in the last resort the indivisible trinity—as Keats is the poet of beauty. But throughout his work love is equated with power: love is the power that moves the universe; love the law governing all life, resolving all conflict, banishing fear and conquering death. The poets and the prophets have always known it; it is the glorious secret of the life of Christ, the bread that can feed the multitudes, the "one essential health, the final sense that sees without sight and hears where no word is spoken, the faith that moves mountains,"[1] yet still the devil has power to turn men to sickness rather than health, blind their eyes, deafen their ears, and lead them to misinterpret and blaspheme the power which is God.

In his last poem,[2] almost his last words, Browning, "ever a fighter," wrote his final message to the world:

Then life is—to wake, not sleep,
Rise and not rest, but press
From earth's level where blindly creep
Things perfected, more or less,
To the heaven's height, far and steep,

Where, amid what strifes and storms
May wait the adventurous quest,
Power is Love—transports, transforms
Who aspired from worst to best,
Sought the soul's world, spurned the worms.

[1] G. Wilson Knight, *The Christian Renaissance*.
[2] *Asolando*.

I have faith such end shall be:
From the first,—Power was—I knew.
Life has made clear to me
That, strive but for closer view,
Love were as plain to see.

Death was for him no disaster; he died, as he lived, splendidly. Mrs. Sutherland Orr, in her *Life and Letters of Robert Browning*, says that

> special signs of physical strength maintained themselves within a few hours of the end. . . . He repeatedly assured his family that he was not suffering.

Like many another great human being, including his own wife, whose last words were: "I feel beautiful," he was given the death he merited, and had surely earned. Blake died composing a poem, or, rather, while singing a song he was composing in the spontaneous way, words and music together, peculiar to himself; Shelley was engulfed by the waves he loved so passionately; a saintly man of recent times, Dr. "Dick" Sheppard, slipped from life to death pen in hand at his writing-desk. It is possible for death to come gently as a friend if it is never feared as an enemy. The poets, the prophets, the saints, have learned to live healthfully, never morbidly, with the thought of death, not "half in love with easeful death" as an escape from a life that has become intolerable, but at peace with the conviction, ratified by the quality of certain transcendent yet still incomplete moments during life, that death will bring these now imperfectly apprehended intuitions to fulfilment. They are vividly aware, too, that death ends finally, irrevocably, all human activities, therefore "let us make haste to live" to love, to do God's work on earth while there is still time.

> Thou oughtest in every action and thought so to order thyself, as if thou wert immediately to die.
>
> . . . .
>
> Be therefore always prepared, and live in such a manner, that death may never find thee unprepared. . . . When that last hour shall come, thou wilt begin to have quite other thoughts of thy whole past life, and be exceeding sorry that thou hast been so negligent and remiss.
>
> How happy and prudent is he who strives now to be such in this life, as he desires to be found at his death. . . .
>
> . . . .
>
> Do now, beloved, do now all thou canst, because thou knowest not when thou shalt die, nor dost thou know what shall befall thee after death.
>
> While thou hast time, gather up for thyself everlasting riches; think of nothing but thy salvation, care for nothing but the things of God.[1]

If the thought of death were inherent in all human relationships, there would be no more agonies of regret and remorse when it is too late to make amends.

[1] Thomas à Kempis, *The Imitation of Christ.*

In *Abt Vogler*, the poem in which art and religion are perfectly merged, Browning writes of the undying power of those we call dead:

> . . . the wonderful Dead who have passed through the
> body and gone,
> But were back once more to breathe in an old world worth
> their new. . . .

They are living again, firing the mind of the musician. And not only the great, the "wonderful" dead, but all who have loved and lived still live, in an even fuller sense, in the lives of those who loved them, with an influence increased by the absence of their bodily presence. Physical proximity is too apt to blind to reality; the true image is blurred, out of perspective; absence strips away many confusing veils; death has the power to remove them all. "I promise you that I will be more perfectly with you and of more use to you, that ever I could be here," said St. Catherine of Siena when she was dying, and this sense of the actual presence of the dead, working, influencing, perfectly loving, is intensely real to millions who have been separated from those they love. There is no need for "spiritualism"; faith and love reveal more than the séance, and God does not need mediums.

> Therefore to whom turn I but to Thee, the ineffable
> Name?
> Builder and maker, Thou, of houses not made with hands!

What, have fear of change from Thee who art ever the
same?
Doubt that Thy power can fill the heart that Thy power
expands?[1]

There shall never be one lost good!
What was, shall live as before;
The evil is null, is nought, is silence implying sound;
What was good, shall be good, with, for evil, so much
good more;
On the earth, the broken arcs; in the heaven, a perfect
round.

Browning, the practical mystic, wrote little or nothing about mysticism or visionary experience in the obvious sense of the word. *Christmas Eve* is the one poem that actually relates a vision. But in *The Strange Medical Experience of Karshish the Arab Physician* the unique position of the mystic in the world is clearly portrayed, although even here in a disguised form. The truth is that Browning was so entirely the true mystic that he shrank from any public demonstration of the fact, just as those with genuine psychic experience would almost deny its existence rather than reply in the affirmative to a commonplace question as to their psychic powers. When real, these are divine secrets that can only be divulged indirectly. Hence, also, Browning's passionate hatred of spiritualism: he knew too much about the real thing to tolerate any counter-

[1] Cf. *Saul*, Stanza XVII, ll. 28, 29.

feit. The story of Lazarus after his resurrection is a precise description of the sufferings and perplexities of the mystic in everyday life. He is set apart; he cannot see with the eyes of other men; they cannot share his vision.

> Whence has this man the balm that brightens all?
> This grown man eyes the world now like a child.

Lazarus folds his hands, and lets them talk, these bewildered men who speculate ignorantly about his condition.

> Heaven opened to a soul while yet on earth,
> Earth forced on a soul's use while seeing Heaven—

How is he to adjust himself? He has lost his sense of proportion, his proper idea of values, they say. Obvious tragedy fails to move him; small things of no account are agony to him.

> The spiritual life around the earthly life:
> The law of that is known to him as this,
> His heart and brain move there, his feet stay here.

Naturally his sense of values cuts right across the values esteemed by the world:

> . . . he knows
> God's secret, while he holds the thread of life.
> Indeed the especial marking of the man
> Is prone submission to the heavenly will.

He owns allegiance to nothing beside. And in him divine love is radiant:

. . . he loves both old and young,
Able and weak, affects the very brutes
And birds—how say I? flowers of the field—
As a wise workman recognises tools
In a master's workshop, loving what they make.

Between the two worlds, "the spiritual life around the earthly life," he hovers in a strange perplexity that is half joy, half agony.

Rabbi Ben Ezra is possibly the most widely known of Browning's religious poems. It is the triumphant poem of courageous old age. Neither age nor death was an enemy to Browning. The young, he believed, have physical beauty and other advantages to compensate for their lack of spiritual understanding, and as the physical powers wane the spiritual powers grow. "Youth shows but half," so it is good to

Rejoice that man is hurled
From change to change unceasingly,
His soul's wings never furled.[1]

Here, again, Browning is the typical Christian psychologist. Psychology is concerned largely with adjustment; the adjustment to different periods in life is often a difficulty, and the right attitude to middle age and old age perhaps the hardest of all. But to the Christian, though there will inevitably be a degree of suffering, there can never be despair, or unhealthy

[1] *James Lee's Wife.*

resistance to the changing demands of life, because all will be seen in the light of development and growth.

> Youth ended, I shall try
> My gain or loss thereby;
> Leave the fire ashes, what survives is gold:
> And I shall weigh the same,
> Give life its praise or blame:
> Youth, all lay in dispute; I shall know, being old
>
> . . . .
>
> So, still within this life
> Though lifted o'er its strife,
> Let me discern, compare, pronounce at last,
> "This rage was right i' the main,
> That acquiescence vain:
> The Future I may face now I have proved the Past."

It is interesting for two reasons to compare the spirit of this poem with another poem about old age written by Mr. Masefield. *Rabbi Ben Ezra* is philosophical, religious, triumphant; Mr. Masefield's poem, *On Growing Old*, is sorrowful, regretful, starved of life or hope. But æsthetically it is the better poem, indicating that in the last resort art has no direct connection with ethics:

> Be with me, Beauty, for the fire is dying,
> My dog and I are old, too old for roving;
> Man, whose young passion sets the spindrift flying,
> Is soon too lame to march, too cold for loving.

I take the book and gather to the fire
Turning old yellow leaves. Minute by minute
The clock ticks to my heart; a withered wire
Moves a thin ghost of music in the spinet.

I cannot sail your seas, I cannot wander
Your mountains, nor your downlands, nor your valleys
Ever again, nor share the battle yonder
Where your young knight the broken squadron rallies;

Only stay quiet, while my mind remembers
The beauty of fire from the beauty of embers.

The spirit of this sonnet is negative; Browning's poem, as usual, positive, still burning with life and the intention to fight to the end, while yet accepting:

Look not thou down but up!

. . . .

So, take and use Thy work!
Amend what flaws may lurk,
What strains o' the stuff, what warpings past the aim!
My times be in Thy hand!
Perfect the cup as planned!
Let age approve of youth, and death complete the
same.

In youth the jig-saw puzzle is scattered about in confusion, nor is it usually possible to glimpse the picture that has to be made; often more than half the span of the threescore years and ten has slipped past before there is any speculation or even thought as to whether there is a picture at all. Then the gathering together of the pieces begins, a laborious and usually painful task. In old age the work is complete, but it remains for death to draw the curtain that always hides the finished puzzle. We build blindfold, except in certain rare moments.

Rabbi Ben Ezra is also the magnificent poem of success in failure:

Not on the vulgar mass
Called "work" must sentence pass,
Things done, that took the eye and had the price;
O'er which, from level stand,
The low world laid its hand,
Found straightway to its mind, could value in a trice.

But all, the world's coarse thumb
And finger failed to plumb,
So passed in making up the main account;
All instincts immature,
All purposes unsure,
That weighed not as his work, yet swelled the man's amount,
Thoughts hardly to be packed
Into a narrow act,
Fancies that broke through language and escaped;
All I could never be,
All, men ignored in me,
This, I was worth to God, whose wheel the pitcher shaped.

The success or failure of a man's life can only be judged by God, "to Whom all hearts are open, all desires known, and from Whom no secrets are hid." The pronouncements of the world cannot be other than short-sighted, if not wholly blind, and concerned with temporal values only. Ignorance and fear are the twin gaolers keeping the prison whence only a few escape. A careful study of Browning would save many a visit to a psycho-therapist: the word "poet" meant originally "maker," and with reason; they are not only makers of beautiful word-designs, but the true builders, having the power to build human souls. And Browning wrote in the dedication to *Sordello:*

> . . . the development of a soul: little else is worth study. I, at least, always thought so—you, with many known and unknown to me, think so—others may, one day.

CONCLUSION

NEVER in history has there been a period when events have moved with such startling rapidity as at the present time. In literature, in theology, in politics, in science, pronouncements are no sooner made than they are out of date. Already, since the Introduction to this book was written, there are strong indications that, in spite of the tragic and disquieting events in many European countries, the Christian revolution may yet come in time to save civilization. Already the younger poets of the modernist school are undergoing radical changes both in their approach to life and in their manner of expression, discovering the invariable rule that in youth the individual experiments with life while in maturity life experiments with the individual, a sobering realization which brings its own measure of despair, surrender, and determination. The older writers of this same school have with one accord affirmed their belief in Christianity as the only hope for a world in chaos. There is a dramatic Renaissance afoot, counterbalancing the pagan and secular movements threatening Europe's peace. This revolution was foreshadowed five years ago by Mr. G. Wilson Knight in his brilliant prophetic book *The Christian Renaissance*. Since then the development has been so rapid and so far-reaching that already the

Christian position in literature has become the truly respectable one: a list of names including Mr. T. S. Eliot, Mr. Aldous Huxley, Mr. Wilson Knight, Mr. John Macmurray, Mr. Middleton Murry and Mr. Michael Roberts, to mention only a few, is formidable, and a conclusive proof of the power of the Christian leaven.

As a natural result, methods of criticism will be overturned, and certain critics recently considered infallible by their followers will find themselves superseded by a more generous, charitable and constructive school which attends primarily to the spirit and approach, the flesh and blood, of a work of art, and only secondly to the technique, the skeleton on which the work is built. When this new school (which is something beyond ordinary criticism, something passionately imaginative and perceptive) is finally established, Browning will inevitably come into his own again. In fact, no poet or writer will be summarily dismissed; there will be a sincere attempt to penetrate to the inner meaning of the work, to share, as far as possible, in the artist's apprehensions, descending to the mysterious depths where the creative process functions. This is all diametrically opposed to the kind of criticism that has prevailed in the last twenty years. It seems now that the literary drought, the period of excessive dryness and destructive intellectuality, is about to be followed by a rich and colourful fertility.

The successful return of religious drama to the stage is further evidence. Mr. Eliot's *Murder in the Cathedral*, and *The Zeal of Thy House*, by a writer known hitherto only for her "thrillers," Miss Dorothy Sayers, are powerful spiritual dramas, and another recent play, *The First Legion*, concerned chiefly with the problem of miracles, and life in a Jesuit community, made an almost popular appeal. All these tendencies provide an effective answer to, for example, the equivocal position taken by Dr. Reinhold Niebuhr in his book, *An Interpretation of Christian Ethics*. His doctrine of mild despair—"It is certain that every achievement will remain in the realm of approximation. The ideal in its perfect form lies beyond the capacities of human nature"—is on the way to being refuted. An ideal logically presupposes achievement, otherwise the idea could never have originated. Ultimately, we create what we believe, and we cannot believe in impossibilities. Dr. Niebuhr dwells too much on the *impossibility* of the ethical ideal. It is perplexing to find a Christian writer affirming and denying in the same breath. He sees so many sides to every question that he ends by seeing clearly scarcely anything at all; a perilous position too easily reached by the profound and liberal thinker. Paradox inevitably runs riot:

> the law of love is an impossible possibility . . . though man always stands under infinite possibilities and is

potentially related to the totality of existence, he is, nevertheless, a creature of finiteness. . . .

Christ is thus the revelation of the very impossible possibility which the Sermon on the Mount elaborates in ethical terms. . . .

And so on, throughout the book. But Christ said: "The Kingdom of Heaven is within you"; he knew that all he promised was possible; he was too completely the realist to suggest impossibilities:

> If ye have faith as a grain of mustard seed, ye shall say unto this mountain, Remove hence to yonder place; and it shall remove; and nothing shall be impossible unto you.[1]

"If ye have faith," yes, even faith so small as a grain of mustard seed. The tragedy is that faith is lacking, therefore so infinitely little is possible. And yet:

I but open my eyes,—and perfection, no more and no less
In the kind I imagined, full-fronts me, and God is seen God,
In the star, in the stone, in the flesh, in the soul, in the clod.[2]

And Browning's words are echoed by Francis Thompson:

[1] *Gospel according to St. Matthew* xvii. 20.
[2] *Saul.*

The drift of pinions, would we hearken,
Beats at our own clay-shuttered doors.

The angels keep their ancient places;—
Turn but a stone, and start a wing!
'Tis ye, 'tis your estrangéd faces,
That miss the many-splendoured thing.[1]

But we are deaf, and self-imprisoned. We cannot hear. Nevertheless, there are, and have been throughout history, lives that passionately deny "Christian defeatism," eyes that see "perfection, no more and no less," souls that have found the Kingdom of Heaven, and know there is no need to wait for fulfilment beyond death. Browning was a vivid example of the power of God to transform human life. And he believed, while recognizing all the difficulties, that love is the final duty, love "the only good in the world." He never talks of this ideal as an impossible possibility, or a possible impossibility. As for the idea of impossibility, Browning's was the faith that would have affirmed that

"the difficult is that which can be done at once;
the impossible that which takes a little longer."

In any case, how is all this talk of impossibility to be reconciled with Jesus's own statement that "with God all things are possible"?

[1] *The Kingdom of God.*

At this moment the finest thinkers in England, writers, theologians, philosophers, even scientists, and some statesmen, realize that Christianity as a working faith is not only possible, but essential. There remains, however, the difficulty that Christianity as generally presented by the Churches often fails to appeal. If this be so, if orthodox religion is a stumbling-block, a wider, freer faith must arise, founded on the words and works of Jesus himself. The Churches are too greatly at variance to inspire confidence. A house divided against itself, its foundations shaken by the earthquakes of a hundred diversities of opinion, cannot provide a refuge for the perplexed. "To whom then shall we go?" There is only one answer. It will be better to care less about the differences among the "two and seventy jarring sects," and continue undismayed the work Christ ordained for his disciples. Religious controversy never had the power to hinder the work to which Browning knew he was called. Technically a churchman, he yet remained essentially free.

The future of civilization is far from being a matter of politics only, and for that reason literature cannot stand aside. Too often in criticism, literature and life have been divorced, and literature considered in abstraction, but so cold a legal proceeding has no power to annul a divine marriage. Since neither can live without the other, any attempt at separation is finally futile. Europe's case is desperate; there cannot be too long a delay, and it is very much the concern of literature at this moment to play an active part in a drama which threatens to end in tragedy. Carefully surveying the present trend in contemporary literature, the first step of the way is not hard to see.

INDEX

BY THE SAME AUTHOR

THE FUTURE OF POETRY

"A lively indignant work by a Christian poet, rebuking the lack of idealism in present-day critics and poets alike."—*The Criterion.*

"Miss Kenmare is exceedingly worried about the future of poetry. She says: 'The retreat from beauty is precipitate and headlong, and the modern poet who dares to use the word at all is bold indeed.' . . . There are many books of ostensible poetry published which justify her diagnosis."—*Sir John Squire in the Daily Telegraph.*

"One of the sanest and most readable books on modern poetry is Miss Dallas Kenmare's *The Future of Poetry.* This analytical study, though iconoclastic in its immediate effect, should clear the way for finer construction. . . . Under no illusions as to the conditions of poetry to-day, Miss Kenmare realises that 'poetry at the present time is very much alive,' and ends on the note that 'the hope for the future lies with the few poets who are brave enough to serve truth, to write as they must, refusing to follow any fashion or school.' "—*The Poetry Review.*

"A thoughtful study which should pass into the hands of all true poetry-lovers."—*Church of England Newspaper.*

FAREWELL TO TREES AND OTHER POEMS

"In several of her new poems . . . Miss Kenmare celebrates stillness. not merely for itself, but as a gateway to a new world of experience. . . , Her imagery has a spring freshness and evokes an inner world."—*Times Literary Supplement.*

"Dallas Kenmare's new volume of poems will advance her reputation as a poet. . . . Her change in technique may lead to individual development, marking a definite and not abrupt stage in the evolution of a poet who has perception, expression and earnestness."—*The Poetry Review.*

"Miss Kenmare's new book contains the purest poetry."—*John o' London's Weekly.*